CW01305614

Alan Cleaver & Lesley Park 2020

THE CORPSE ROADS OF CUMBRIA

The Corpse Roads of Cumbria

Walks along the county's ancient pathways

Alan Cleaver & Lesley Park

Lakeland Book of the Year winner 2019

Chitty Mouse Press

2020

Credits:

Published by Alan Cleaver and Lesley Park
Chitty Mouse Press, 57 Church Street,
Whitehaven, Cumbria CA28 7EX
Email: alanjcleaver@gmail.com

Our thanks to: Whitehaven Archive & Local Studies Centre, Maureen Fisher, Malcolm Ewart, Jean Altshuler, Jane and Peter Douglas, Gary and Janice Bullivant, Thérèse Chambers; Nick Thorne, Roger Asquith, pixabay.com; Maggie Dickinson; Sylvia Pilling; Rev'd George Wrigley; www.geog.port.ac.uk

The right of Alan Cleaver and Lesley Park to be identified as authors of this work has been asserted in accordance with the Copyright, Designs and Patent Act, 1988.

All rights reserved.

First published February 2018; Second edition: April 2018. Third edition March 2019. This edition January 2020

Ordnance Survey Licence: © Crown copyright and database rights 2019 Ordnance Survey 100055619. © Local Government Information House Limited copyright and database rights 2019 100055619.

Note: The usual orientation of maps is roughly north/south but occasionally we have rotated them to fit better on the page.

Also by Alan Cleaver & Lesley Park: *Get Lost - in the lonnings, trods and ancient paths of Cumbria,* which explores some of the county's lesser known footpaths

NORTH CUMBRIA

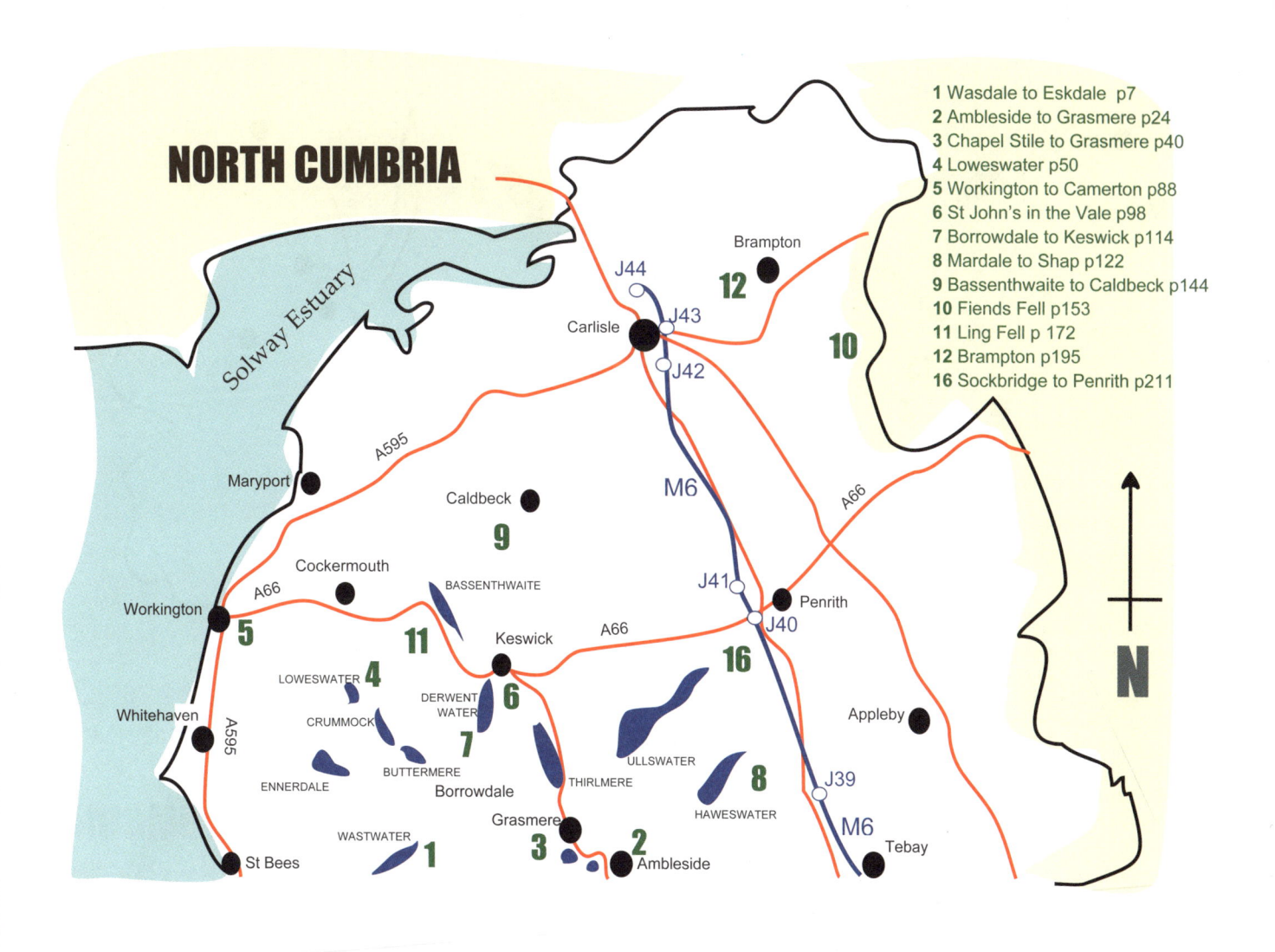

1 Wasdale to Eskdale p7
2 Ambleside to Grasmere p24
3 Chapel Stile to Grasmere p40
4 Loweswater p50
5 Workington to Camerton p88
6 St John's in the Vale p98
7 Borrowdale to Keswick p114
8 Mardale to Shap p122
9 Bassenthwaite to Caldbeck p144
10 Fiends Fell p153
11 Ling Fell p 172
12 Brampton p195
16 Sockbridge to Penrith p211

SOUTH CUMBRIA

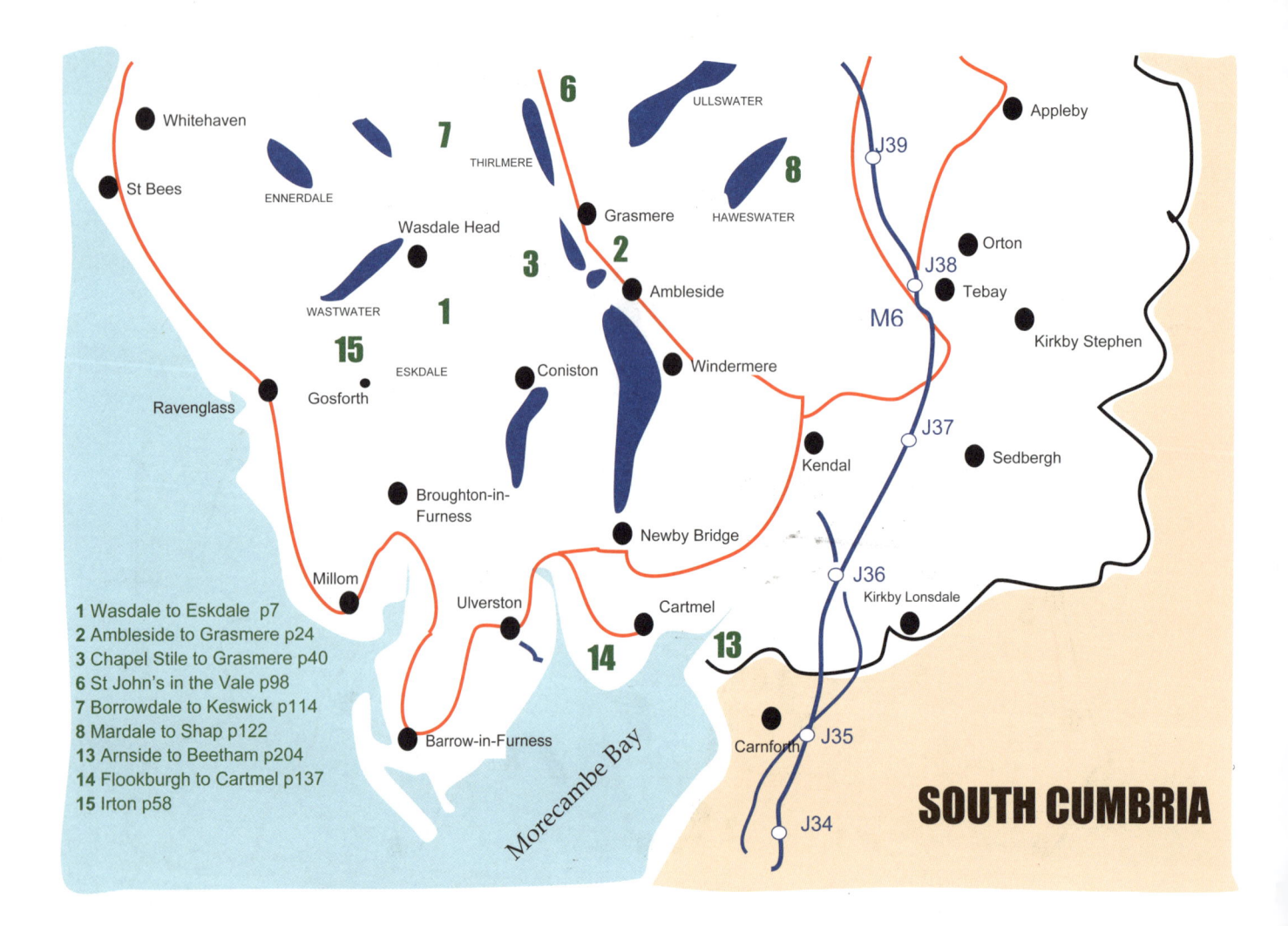

1 Wasdale to Eskdale p7
2 Ambleside to Grasmere p24
3 Chapel Stile to Grasmere p40
6 St John's in the Vale p98
7 Borrowdale to Keswick p114
8 Mardale to Shap p122
13 Arnside to Beetham p204
14 Flookburgh to Cartmel p137
15 Irton p58

Contents

Introduction	1
Wasdale to Eskdale	7
The Walk	22
Ambleside to Grasmere	24
Armitt Map	30
Nab Well	35
The Walk	37
Chapel Stile to Grasmere	40
The Walk	42
Down't Lonnin	48
Loweswater	50
The Walk	54
Maggie's Lonning	56
Irton	58
Irton Oak and Lady Lamplugh	64
Bridal Paths	70
Irton Walk One: Irton Hall	73
Burne-Jones windows	77
Irton Walk Two: Holmrook	78
Irton Walk Three: Stock Bridge	83
Are You Sitting Comfortably?	87
Workington to Camerton	88
The Walk	92
St John's in the Vale	98
The Walk	102
The Night Watch	105

Borrowdale to Keswick	114	Exit Stage Left	170
The Walk	117	Ling Fell	172
Knock, Knock	119	The Walk	176
Mardale to Shap	122	Coffin Rests	178
The Walk	125	Arval Bread & Funeral Feasts	189
Corpse Candles and Death Lights	132	Around Brampton	195
Flookburgh to Cartmel	137	Fenton to Hayton Walk	197
The Walk	138	Irthington Walk	202
Can We All Please Just Cheer Up	141	A Way With The Fairies	204
Bassenthwaite to Caldbeck	144	Beetham Walk	208
Telling The Bees	150	Sockbridge to Penrith	211
Fiends Fell	153	Last Writes	215
The Walk	158	Index	218
You Are Bidden	160		
Greystoke	163		

Introduction

Now it is the time of night,
That the graves all gaping wide,
Every one lets forth his sprite,
In the church-way paths to glide.

— Puck in *Midsummer Night's Dream*

CUMBRIA has a number of corpse roads – a few even marked as such on Ordnance Survey maps and sign-posts. It's generally accepted that such paths – they are normally more path than road – were used to transport the dead in medieval times from a remote church to the 'mother' church. They go by many names including: bier road, burial road, coffin road, coffin line, lyke or lych way, funeral road, procession way, corpse way and so forth, and the concept exists in many cultures around the world. In this country at least, a number of corpse roads seem to have a special significance and are clothed in folklore and superstition, such as tales of ghosts and spectral funeral processions.

The existence of corpse roads asks many questions. Why transport a body several miles to a church instead of just burying it locally? If every path taken by a coffin became a corpse road surely that would make every path and road a 'corpse road'? And if most roads were corpse roads, why do some survive with a special mythology all of their own? How were the bodies transported: Did mourners carry the coffin on their shoulders all those miles, only stopping to rest at an occasional 'coffin-rest'? Or was it strapped to a horse in some bizarre fashion? These questions and more occurred to my partner Lesley and I as we began to walk and research these ancient

The famous – but faint – corpse road from Mardale to Shap

paths. Our original intention was to produce a book of walks following these corpse roads (we produced a similar book on lonnings – a Cumbrian dialect term for country lanes – in 2013) but the routes are inextricably linked with the customs and superstitions surrounding death so the book also looks at the funereal traditions of Westmorland and Cumberland (the two counties merged in 1974 to form Cumbria).

It sounds a morbid subject but we hope it is more fascinating than melancholic and felt in any case it was important to record many of these customs in one volume. Knowing which questions to ask is one thing; finding the answers is the devil's own job. The true purpose of corpse roads is all but lost to written records and any oral tradition passed down through generations has become hopelessly garbled. We can perhaps be certain that the original purpose was to carry the dead from remote villages to the 'mother' church which had a licence for burials. The 'hey-day' for corpse roads was probably early medieval times. By the 18th Century most churches had won the right to bury their dead locally rather than send them to a distant mother church.

Written records are rare but we know, for example, from church records that until the late 16th Century the inhabitants of Killington and Firbank in east Cumbria had to bury their dead at Kirkby Lonsdale church some 10 miles away. We can therefore presume that the main path between their parish and the church was a 'corpse road' – but can't be sure. In 1585, in a petition similar to that written by many other parishes around this time, they asked the Bishop to allow them to have the same religious rights of Sacrament, Divine Service and burial at Killington chapel "by reason of their distance from the parish church (some of them being distant ten miles and none less than six), and by reason of inundations and of storms frequently raging in those parts in the winter season, they cannot carry their dead to be buried without great trouble and inconvenience, nor their children to be baptised without great peril both of soul and body, nor resort thither to hear divine service and receive the sacraments as becometh christians, and by right

'The best attended ceremony is that of a funeral. At one time the bellman went round, to announce that on a certain day and hour so-and-so would be buried at such a place. This custom still lingers. Perhaps one or two hundred persons may accompany the corpse of a neighbour to church, most of whom never attend a place of worship at other times'

– *The History and Topography of the Counties of Cumberland and Westmoreland*, edited by William Whellan, 1860

The snow-covered corpse road that stretches from Chapel Stile to Grasmere

they are bounden". Their petition was successful.

The hey-day of newspapers was in the late 19th Century and the Victorian antiquarian revival was mid-19th Century so it's from around 1830 onwards that we start to get written records of corpse roads. Prior to this we are forced to examine a few shadows, fading footprints and famously unreliable oral traditions. In some ways what is worse is the authoritative tone of many of the authors of today's folklore books who claim definitive knowledge on the subject but are unable to give any sources for these 'facts'. When some church leaflet describes the route of a corpse road, or a tourist sign points out a coffin rest we find ourselves asking 'Yes, but how do you know?'.

To be fair, our background is journalism so we're often no better – preferring to tell a good tale rather than get bogged down in thesis-style academia. But we'll strive to at least give the earliest source possible for some of the legends.

When we began our research in 2016, you could quickly lay your hands on perhaps eight known corpse roads in Cumbria. The internet and guide books listed the likes of Mardale, Wasdale, Grasmere and Loweswater with the usual vague explanation that the paths were used in the past to carry the dead. Our research included a trawl of the archives to eke out some of the long, lost roads. We were helped in our quest by the good work currently being done by the likes of Google in digitising old books that have long since vanished from library shelves. And those books would often mention other 'lost' books that have perhaps not yet been digitised but could be found somewhere in the real world. The good folk of Cumbria were also kind enough to volunteer their own suggestions but we felt reluctant to include all of these unless we could find a written source giving some credence or age to the local oral tradition. It's been a fascinating project with the added advantage of having somewhere with a purpose to walk at the weekends. And as the project grew to include funereal traditions, it opened up a rich seam of stories from the older generation as they recalled the customs and folklore surrounding the death of a member of the family. It's only a pity a book of this nature wasn't written

> One of the earliest newspaper accounts of corpse roads...
>
> **Deaths:** On the 7th inst, at Pikeside, in Ulpha, Tamar, wife of Mr Myles Whinfield, aged 86. Owing to the great fall of snow, the corpse was obliged to be carried by a footpath, about 120 years ago used as the regular corpse road, but never since, except once about 60 years ago, the general cart road having been entirely blocked up, as is the case now.
>
> **– Whitehaven Herald**
> **Sunday, 22 March 1835**

some 200 years ago when there was still access to those who remembered the use of corpse roads.

The one exception to the vague mist of the history of corpse roads is the village of Irton. The corpse roads there were the subject of a lengthy court battle in 1899. This put the roads under sharp scrutiny, mapping out their precise route and their history.

Sadly for the most part we have no such detailed records for corpse roads and must rely on myths, legends and ghost stories. Or we are faced with a path marked 'Old Corpse Road' on OS Maps (such as the one at Ling Fell) but can find no other evidence or information. Perhaps the best evidence is from those interviews with the wise old men and women of the village who could at least recall an oral tradition of a corpse road route.

We are reminded of a short extract from *The Whitehaven Herald* which shows just how powerful the combination of written and oral records can be. The cutting is dated 1850 – so the starting point is 167 years ago. It then quotes a man who said that 30 years ago (ie 1820) he spoke to a man who was 109 years old (1711) and this centenarian had been told by his grandfather (so we're now back to the mid 1600s) that the stone circle in Lowther Castle, Whitehaven had been dismantled and the stones used in Cartgate Mansion and other places. So that's 400 years back in time in just one sentence!

Further reading

A good introduction to the subject is *Spirit Roads: An Exploration of Otherworldly Routes* by Paul Devereux. It gives a global view of the topic and details how spirit roads are reflected in other cultures.

Roads and Tracks of the Lake District by Brian Paul Hindle gives a scholarly overview of the whole topic of trackways throughout history in Cumbria.

Wasdale to Eskdale

A challenging walk which comes complete with a ghost

> "It was at this time that I learned of a similar occasion at Cleator Moor not long before, when the corpse was taken out of the coffin and stood up in a corner whilst the merriment was going on. He was an 'uninterested' onlooker."
>
> — **John W Skelly,** *Back to the 1920s*

THIS is one of the more famous corpse roads in Cumbria but few are aware of the origin of the ghost story that is associated with it. The corpse road stretches from Wasdale Head to the village of Boot in Eskdale (and on to St Catherine's Church a few hundred yards further on towards the river). This account from the website *Mysterious Britain* gives a typical overview of the road and legend:

"As Wasdale had no church early in its history, the deceased had to be carried over the fells to Eskdale for interment, and this route became known as the corpse road. This is haunted by the ghost of a horse carrying the body of woman tied to it. Her son had died and whilst his body was being carried from Wasdale over the corpse road to Eskdale the horse carrying his body bolted and was lost in the mist. His mother died shortly after, never recovering from the loss of *her son or that of his body. As she was being carried along the road the horse was lost in a snow storm and never seen again. Although the son's body was subsequently found, the mother is left and haunts alone."*

The route (marked as the Old Corpse Road on Cumbria's definitive map but not on the Ordnance Survey map) stretches from the Wasdale Head Inn, past Burnmoor Tarn (passing a lovely double-backed packhorse bridge en route) before eventually dropping down into Eskdale past Boot Mill. It is a long walk and one which at times takes you through boggy terrain but it's not impossible to get there and back in one day. Most folk, however, may prefer to start from either end and walk as far as Burnmoor Tarn before turning back.

The curious double-backed packhorse bridge at Wasdale Head (NY184 068)

Burnmoor Tarn – the halfway point on the Wasdale to Eskdale corpse road

St Catherine's Church is down Church Lonning, dates from around the 14th Century and was restored in 1881. According to legend, the church may have once existed further east somewhere in the vicinity of St Catherine's holy well. Water from this well has been used within living memory for baptisms at the church. St Catherine's well is not easy to find and farmer Noel Baines led a party of enthusiasts to the site in 2010 and told how he had used water from the well at the baptism of his grandson Stephen 12 years previously. The grid reference for the well is NY 181 003. Signposts have recently been erected and there is a map at the church showing directions. Until the church was licensed for burials, villagers themselves needed a corpse road which led to St Bees. A church leaflet published a few years ago for St Catherine's states:

"In 1445 the people of Eskdale petitioned the Pope complaining of the hardships of the journey to St Bees for baptisms, burials and the sacraments. In the 10-mile journey, they said, there were broad waters, mountains and streams which were often in flood. The petition was referred to the Abbot of Calder Abbey to deal with as he thought fit by the Holy See. He was instructed, if the facts were true, to erect ie promote the chapel to a parish church with burial ground, font, bell tower and bells and other parochial insignia after due compensation for loss of revenue had been paid to the mother church of St Bees."

The reference to 'loss of revenue' relates to the fee that churches could expect to claim for performing burials. A reluctance of Mother churches to give up this source of income may account for the extended use of corpse roads during the Middle Ages.

Before returning to the ghost, it is worth recording one other humorous story about the corpse road; a tale probably invented by Auld Will Ritson (1808 – 1890), the 19th Century landlord of the Hunstman Inn (now the Wasdale Head Inn) and famed storyteller. Author Thomas Ellwood (1838 – 1911) tells in his book, *Landnama Book of Iceland as it illustrates the dialect, place names, folklore, & antiquities of Cumberland, Westmorland, and North Lancashire*, how he was once told this story by Will Ritson:

St Catherine's holy well, Eskdale. It's about a quarter of a mile east of the church at NY181 003

The bleak Wasdale to Eskdale corpse road

"It has from time immemorial been the custom of the people of Wasdale to carry their dead to Eskdale or Netherwasdale Church for interment, there being no burial ground attached to the church at Wasdale Head. The corpse in the coffin is slung over the back of a horse and carried in this fashion over the fell. On one occasion (lang sen) the wife of a dalesman was being so carried for interment when upon the edge of the fell the coffin, through the negligence of the driver of the horse, came in contact with a rowan tree, and was thrown to the ground. By the concussion the coffin was forced open, and the supposed corpse was found to be alive. She returned home with her friends, and lived for several years after. When she died, and the same kind of cavalcade was following her remains in very much the same fashion, as they approached the said rowan tree again, her husband, who was bringing up the rear, called out (according to Will) in stentorian tones : 'Tak' care o' that rowan tree!' This time, however, the rowan tree was successfully cleared."

The use of rowan in the story is suggestive as this was a tree which, in the 19th Century, was believed to have magical properties and was usually used as a form of protection against witches and witchcraft. In Whitehaven, for example, antiquarian 'Putty Joe' Hodgson tells how at Halloween people would tie a piece of rowan to their front doors to keep witches away.

Unusually, we have been able to trace the origin of the ghost that haunts the Wasdale to Eskdale corpse road. It was first written down by Victorian author Hall Caine (1853-1931). As a young boy, Hall stayed with his

In Westmorland also the idea in the value of corpse roads still lingers. Not long ago at Appleby an applicant who wished the magistrates to order some repairs to be done to a cart track on the fells urged in support of his plea that "the road had been used as a funeral road," and so was essentially public.

— *Yorkshire Post* March 10 1899

grandfather at Sowermyrr Farm, Wasdale Head and it was he who regaled the young Hall with the tale. The story so excited and inspired Hall that he determined one day to write it down. He used it as the core of his novel, *The Shadow of a Crime*, published in 1885. Hall wrote on more than one occasion about the origin of the story including in *My First Book* in 1892. This was a collection of interviews with famous authors about their start in publishing. So here is the original corpse road ghost story as told by Hall Caine:

The most famous person you have never heard of…

IT is hard to comprehend just how famous Hall Caine was in his day – particularly because today no one has heard of him. His novel, *The Eternal City*, was the world's first million selling novel and he was the highest-paid novelist of his day. Crowds would gather outside his house in the hope of catching a glimpse of him and he was once mobbed in New York. He was rated alongside Dickens and Tolstoy. His novel, *The Manxman* was the last silent film made by Alfred Hitchcock. On Caine's death, King George V led the condolences. Over 60,000 people attended his funeral on the Isle of Man and a memorial service was also held in London attended by the great and the good. So why did he so quickly pass into obscurity? It seems his Victorian style is simply 'out of fashion'. But it's rather ironic that while Caine is forgotten the ghost he conjured up lives on.

Hall Caine: The first to record the ghost story

- Caine also lived for a short time in Keswick

MY first novel may very properly be regarded as my first book, and if I have no tale to tell of heart-broken impediments in getting it published, I have something to say of the difficulty of getting it written. The novel is called *The Shadow of a Crime*, but title it had none until it was finished, and a friend christened it. I cannot remember when the story was begun, because I cannot recall a time when the idea of it did not exist in my mind. I think it must be in the nature of imagination that an imaginative idea does not spring into being, that it has no spontaneous generation, but, as a germinating conception, a shadow of a vision, always comes floating from somewhere out of the back chambers of memory. You are waiting for the central thought that shall link together incidents that you have gleaned from among the stubble of many fields, for the motif that shall put life and meaning into the characters that you have gathered and grouped, and one morning, as you awake, just at that moment when you are between the land of light and the mists of sleep, and as your mind is grappling back for the vanishing form of some delicious dream, a dim but familiar ghost of an idea comes up unbidden for the hundredth time, and you say to yourself, with surprise at your own stupidity, 'That's it !'

The idea of my first novel moved about me in this way for many years before I recognised it. As usually happens, it came in the shape of a story. I think it was, in actual fact, first of all, a tale of a grandfather. My mother's father was a Cumberland man, and he was full of the lore of the hills and dales. One of the oldest legends of the Lake mountains tells of the time of the plague. The people were afraid to go to market, afraid to meet at church, and afraid to pass on the highway. When any lonely body was ill, the nearest neighbour left meat and drink at the door of the afflicted house, and knocked and ran away. In these days, a widow with two sons lived in one of the darkest of the valleys. The younger son died, and the body had to be carried over the mountains to be buried. Its course lay across Sty Head Pass, a bleak and 'brant' place, where the winds are often high. The eldest son, a strong-hearted lad, undertook the duty. He strapped the coffin on to the back of a young horse, and they started away. The day was wild, and on the top of the pass, where the path dips into Wastdale, between the breast of Great Gable and the heights of Scawfell, the wind rose to a gale. The horse was terrified. It broke away and galloped over the fells, carrying its burden with it. The lad followed and searched for it, but in vain, and he had to go home at last, unsatisfied. This was in the spring, and nearly all the summer through the surviving son of the widow was out on the mountains, trying to recover the runaway horse, but never once did he catch sight of it, though sometimes, as he turned homeward at night, he thought he heard, in the gathering darkness, above the sough of the wind, the horse's neigh. Then winter came, and the mother died. Once more the dead body had to be carried over the fells for burial, and once again the coffin was strapped on the back of a horse. It was an old mare that was chosen this time, the mother of the young one that had been lost. The snow lay deep on the pass, and from the cliffs of the Scawfell pikes it hung in great toppling masses. All went well with the little funeral party until they came to the top of the pass, and though the day was dead calm the son held the rein with a hand that was like a vice.

"Its fascination for me lay in its shadow and suggestion of the supernatural. I thought it had all the grip of a ghost story without ever passing out of the world of reality"

— Hall Caine

But just as the mare reached the spot where the wind had frightened the young horse, there was a terrific noise. An immense body of the snow had parted at that instant from the beetling heights overhead, and rushed down into the valley with the movement as of a mighty earthquake, and the deafening sound as of a peal of thunder. The dale echoed and re-echoed from side to side, and from height to height. The old mare was affrighted; she reared, leapt, flung her master away, and galloped off. When they had recovered from their consternation, the funeral party gave chase, and at length, down in a hollow place, they thought they saw what they were in search of. It was a horse with something strapped on its back. When they came up with it they found it was the young horse, with the coffin of the younger son. They led it away and buried the body that it had carried so long, but the old mare they never recovered, and the body of the mother never found sepulchre. Such was the legend, sufficiently terrible, and even ghastly, which was the germ of my first novel. Its fascination for me lay in its shadow and suggestion of the supernatural. I thought it had all the grip of a ghost story without ever passing out of the world of reality. Imagination played about the position of that elder son, and ingenuity puzzled itself for the sequel to his story. What did he think? What did he feel? What were his superstitions? What became of him? Did he die mad, or was he a man, and did he rise out of all doubt and terror? I cannot say how many years this ghost of a conception (with

St Michael's Church, Nether Wasdale – described by the Carlisle Diocese as originally a chapel of ease to the parish of St Bees Priory

various brothers and sisters of a similar complexion) haunted my mind before I recognised it as the central incident of a story, the faggot for a fire from which other incidents might radiate and imaginary characters take life."

There are some interesting points to note in Hall Caine's account. First, he was told this story by his grandfather so it places the story at least in the late 18th Century. This means it's not impossible for it to have literally been a story handed down since the time of plague (late 17th Century). Secondly, the tale is not associated with a corpse road from Wasdale to Eskdale, rather one going over the Sty Head Pass. One wonders at what point the story 'moved' the few miles across the fells. It's difficult to see why a corpse road would exist over Sty Head Pass to Wasdale since our research says the people of

St Olaf's Church at Wasdale Head

Borrowdale took their coffins to Crosthwaite, near Keswick. Perhaps it just made for a better tale for a man to tell his grandson.

St Olaf's Church is the one that sits at the bottom of Sty Head Pass and is famously England's smallest church in the valley with the deepest lake, the tallest mountain – and the biggest liar. Historic England record the first mention of a chapel on this site as 1550 but it was not consecrated until 1901. And it was not given a name (dedication) until 1977 when the Bishop of Carlisle dedicated the church to St Olaf. It is today considered the 'mountaineers' church' being a spot of spiritual solace for those about to climb Scafell Pike or for those who have just returned. Poignantly it is also the burial place for many unfortunate climbers who have lost their lives on the mountains. Interestingly, the report of the consecration makes a point of saying that burials would now be possible at the church instead of at St Michael's Church, Nether Wasdale. This church was consecrated as far back as 1535 and the earliest burial still extant is dated 1785 so one presumes the people of Wasdale were buried here rather than being taken over a tortuous corpse

The iconic packhorse bridge at Wasdale Head

road over Eskdale Moor to Boot. There are a couple more reasons to be suspicious of the Wasdale to Eskdale corpse road. MJB Baddeley in *The Thorough Guide to the English Lake District* (1880) suggests this path only became a public road around 1870. And there is a personal reminiscence in *Annales Caermoelenses, Or Annals of Cartmel* published in 1872 which dates back to the mid 18th Century which says the dead of Wasdale were buried at Nether Wasdale:

"In west Cumberland, where the mountains are so precipitous, and the roads so steep and difficult, a lady, who died in Ulverstone in 1867, in her 90th year, and who was a baby in arms, at Whitehaven, when Paul Jones bombarded that town in 1788, used to relate that when she was young, an old woman told her that she could remember corpses being brought out of Wasdale in winding sheets, across the backs of horses, for interment at Strand, a village at the foot of Wastwater; there being then no roads but pack-horse tracks in those parts."

It seems our corpse road has vanished into the mists as mysteriously as the spectral horse.

Further reading

Annales Caermoelenses, Or Annals of Cartmel – James Stockdale, 1872

If you can find a copy, seek out *The Vikings, Wasdale Head and Their Church – A Historical Chronicle, Maybe True – Maybe Not* by Bill Bailey, 2002

When visiting Eskdale, watch out for the *Discover Eskdale* range of booklets featuring local walks.

Journey's end: St Catherine's Church at the end of Church Lonning, Eskdale — and the end of the corpse road

Wasdale to Eskdale

Distance: 10km – and another 10km back!

Map: OL6 – Explorer

Difficulty: This is a tough route across some difficult terrain and involving steep climbs. You need to be prepared for fell walking with the right clothing, a map and compass (and knowledge of how to use them) and walk in the summer when you have more daylight hours. You may prefer to walk half way along the route (say to Burnmoor Tarn) and then turn back.

Start: You can start at either end. There is parking at Wasdale Head with food and drink available at the Wasdale Head Inn. If you start from the Eskdale end, you can park at Dalegarth station and there are a number of pubs in Boot.

Things to see en route:
Britain's Favourite View (NY150 053). Stand at the western end of Wastwater and look east. This is Britain's Favourite View according to a poll taken in 2007 by viewers of ITV. But almost any view in this part of the world would equal it.

Wasdale Head Packhorse bridge (Row bridge): (NY186 088) Almost photographed as much as Ashness Bridge near Keswick. This one is a lot prettier but is probably not so famous as it is rather 'remote'. You will find it near the Wasdale Head Inn.

Double packhorse bridge: (NY184 068) Packhorse bridges are synonymous with the Lake District but this one is very unusual in being a 'double' bridge (See p8).

St Olaf's Church: (NY188 086). The 'mountaineers' church' as it sadly is the final resting place for a number of climbers who have lost their lives on the fells.

Burnmoor Tarn (NY184 044). A hauntingly beautiful tarn halfway across the fell.

Boot Mill: (NY176 011) A historic watermill.

St Catherine's holy well: (NY181 003) About quarter of a mile east of St Catherine's Church, Eskdale. It is signposted but is not easy to find (See picture p10).

The La'al Ratty: A narrow gauge steam engine that runs from Dalegarth to Ravenglass. Its name is dialect for the little Ratty.

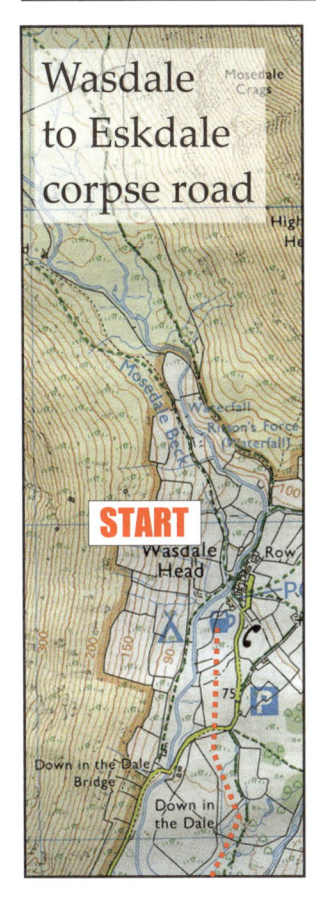

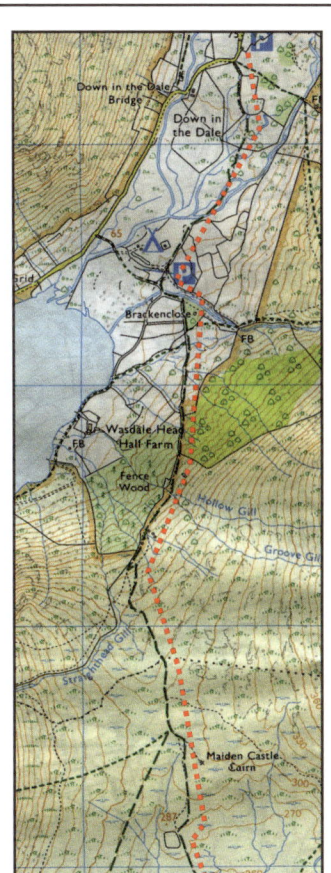

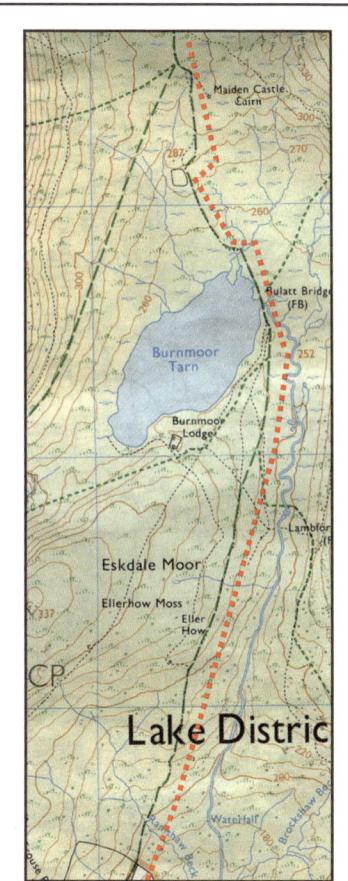

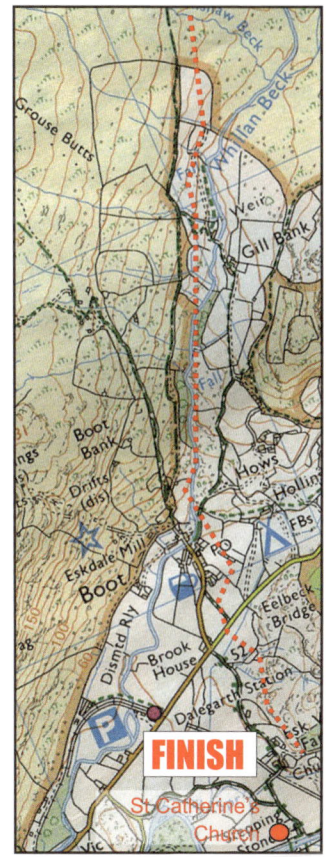

THE CORPSE ROADS OF CUMBRIA

WASDALE TO ESKDALE : 23

Wasdale to Eskdale corpse road

START

FINISH

Ambleside to Grasmere

A popular path following in the footsteps of William and Dorothy Wordsworth

> 'From every hamlet or homestead to the parish church was a particular road or path called a corpse road and so exact were they on these occasions to keep upon that path that in time of flood a funeral party has been known to wade knee deep through the water rather than deviate a few yards to the right or left.'
>
> — John Richardson, 1876

THIS is one of the more famous — and popular — corpse roads in Cumbria offering tourists an easy walk from Rydal Mount where Wordsworth lived from 1813 until his death in 1850, past Dove Cottage — the poet's former home — and to St Oswald's Church, Grasmere. It officially starts in Ambleside but the road from there and along the drive through Rydal Hall are rather dull and most people start at Rydal Mount. Along with the Mardale corpse road it is one of the two that are actually signposted 'corpse road' and along the way you will pass a couple of coffin rests, stones where mourners would apparently 'rest' en route to the church.

But who first claimed this was a corpse road and that these were coffin rests? Neither William nor Dorothy Wordsworth – who spent most of their lives living on the corpse road and writing about the landscape – mention them. You would think they might have jotted down a note or composed a poem about the corpse road going past their front door. The earliest published reference appears in 1912 in *The Church of Grasmere* by Mary Armitt (published posthumously) when she talks about paths taken by people going to worship at St Oswald's. Her description of the church and corpse roads are difficult to follow and her map included in the book is equally frustrating to decipher. We have reprinted both for you to chew over!

She refers to "the Ambleside folk, when in 1674 they petitioned their Bishop for the right of burial in their chapel, stated that 'by reason of the heat in summer and the great snowes and sudden inundations of water in winter it is very difficult and dangerous to carry their dead thither (to Grasmere) for burial'." This ties in with many other medieval

The corpse road between Rydal Mount and Grasmere

references to funeral routes and dates their first references to petitions to Bishops calling for more local burials. Although the Wordsworths pointedly don't refer to any corpse roads in their journals, we can be grateful to Dorothy for an early description of a funeral in Grasmere which makes reference to the cortege stopping at various points for reading of psalms or hymns:

Rydal Mount: The former home of the Wordsworths. Yet they never mentioned the corpse road that passed their house

Wednesday, 3rd September 1800:
A fine coolish morning. I ironed till half past three – now very hot. I then went to a funeral at John Dawson's. About 10 men and four women. Bread cheese and ale. They talked sensibly and cheerfully about common things. The dead person 56 years of age buried by the parish. The coffin was neatly lettered and painted black and covered with a decent cloth. They set the corpse down at the door and while we stood within the threshold the men with their hats off sang with decent and solemn countenances a verse of a funeral psalm. The corpse was then borne down the hill and they sang till they had got past the Town-end. I was affected to tears while we stood in the house, the coffin lying before me. There were no near kindred, no children. When we got out of the dark house, the sun was shining and the prospect looked so divinely beautiful as I never saw it. It seemed more sacred than I had ever seen it, and yet more allied to human life.

A 'coffin rest' on the Grasmere corpse road adapted as a memorial seat

The coffin rest near to Dove Cottage

The green fields, neighbours of the churchyard, were as green as possible and with the brightness of the sunshine looked quite gay. I thought she was moving to a quiet spot and I could not help weeping very much. When we came to the bridge they began to sing again and stopped during four lines before they entered the churchyard. The priest met us – he did not look as a man ought to do on such an occasion – I had seen him half-drunk the day before in a pot-house."

The route from Dove Cottage and Town-end to St Oswald's would, by necessity, have used what is now called the coffin route. We have here also mention of other funeral customs including the food and drink offered, and the removal of hats (at other times and places it has been considered more polite for men to keep hats on).

And what of the coffin rests on this corpse road? It has to be said both are unconvincing. The one on the route below Nab Scar has been converted into a seat. The one nearer to Dove Cottage is strangely small. We are yet to find out who – and on what evidence – first put a sign up declaring this was indeed a coffin rest. The sign currently says:

"Coffin Stone" or "Resting Stone" – Before St Mary's Church in Ambleside was consecrated, coffins had to be transported along the 'corpse road' from Ambleside 4km to St Oswald's Church at Grasmere for burial. This route is now the present day bridle path to Rydal. This stone along with others along the way was used for supporting

Tourists on the corpse road pass the neglected Nab Well, near Rydal Mount,

the coffin while the bearers rested. Another corpse road over Hunting Stile and Red Bank was used to bring coffins over for burial from Chapel Stile, Great Langdale, until The Holy Trinity Church and graveyard was consecrated in 1821."

We suspect it was Mary Armitt who suggested this as a coffin rest – or someone who had read Armitt's *The Church of Grasmere* talks. She wrote about "a huge stone standing on the line was known as the How Stone" and says that at How Top "there is still a flat-topped boulder used for resting burdens upon". The coffin rest is a bit below How Top but without more specifics it's hard to rule definitively on the subject. More clues were given by Armitt in a talk she gave shortly before her death. She told an audience at Carlisle on 27th April 1905: *"The house-holders above Stock (Ambleside) had to turn their steps for worship, to carry their babes for baptism and their dead for burial three or four miles up the valley to Grasmere Churchyard, by the high track under Nab Scar. At various stations on the way, according to tradition, it was the custom to rest the coffins on large stones while the bearers were changed. The Howe stone on the south side of White Moss has disappeared. But one on the north side still lies by the road under a tree, and is used now by the carrier for the dropping of parcels for adjacent houses."*

Frustratingly the "north side" of White Moss "by the road under a tree" is too vague to be sure if it's the one now signposted as the coffin rest.

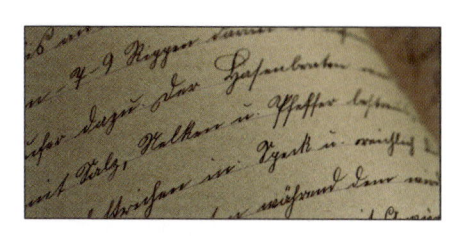

Further reading

The Church of Grasmere by Mary Armitt (1912). Available from Sam Read's Bookshop in Grasmere.

At Lakeland's Heart by John M Carnie. An indispensable if slightly romantic history of Ambleside. Available from Fred's Bookshop, Ambleside

If Nab Well inspires you to seek out holy wells and sacred springs in the Cumbrian landscape then search out Fr John Musther's book, *Springs of Living Waters.*

30 : AMBLESIDE TO GRASMERE

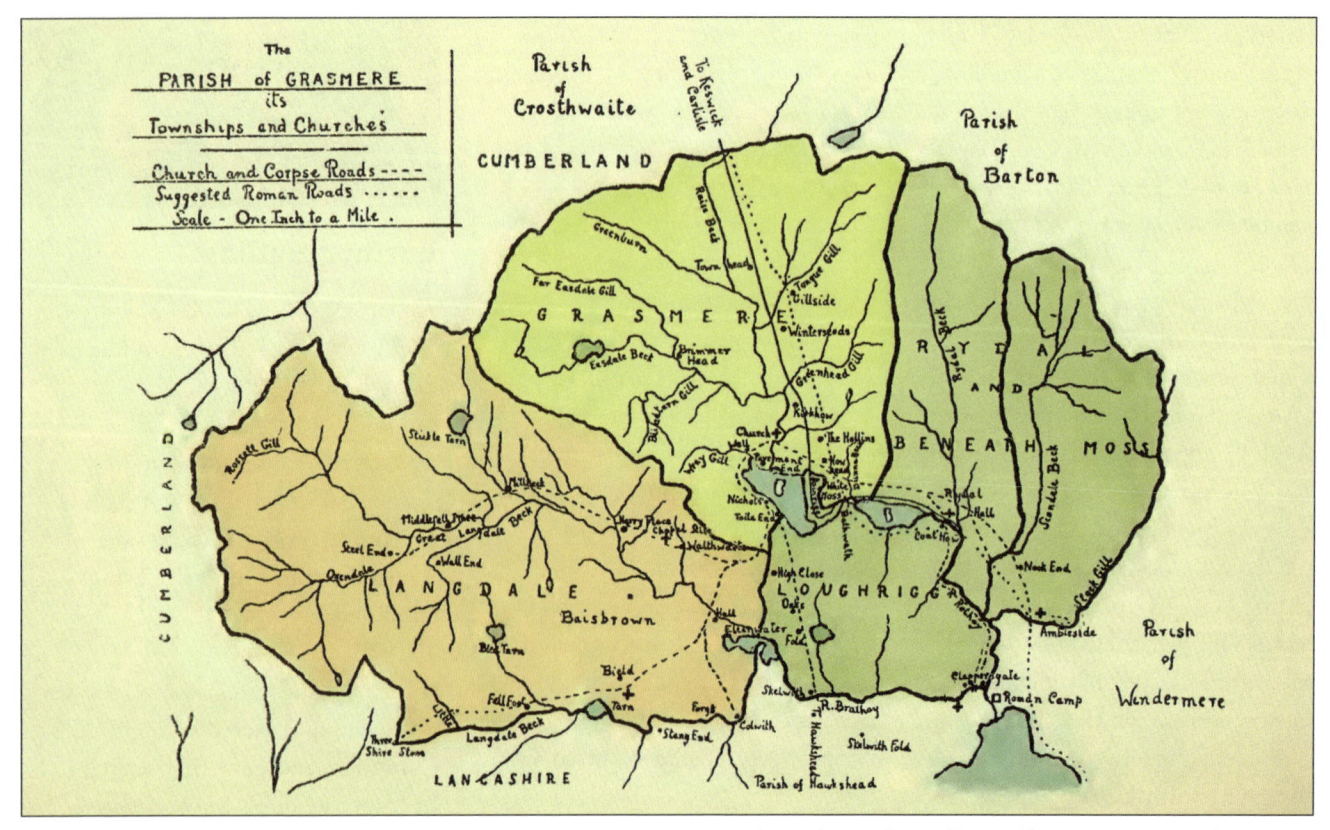

The map published in *The Church of Grasmere* by Mary Armitt in 1912. Also online at https://goo.gl/8L92Gy

THE ARMITT MAP

We are reproducing the map of Grasmere's corpse roads and paths that was first published in 1912 in *The Church of Grasmere* by Mary Armitt (See previous page). The book is out of print so we are also reproducing her accompanying text. Both are rather confused but it is the first detailed account of the village's corpse roads. The confusion is not helped by the decision of the book's editor to include a lengthy footnote rather than include it in the main text. The book also does not say what is the source of her statements. The book was published posthumously.

Mary and her two sisters (Sophia and Annie) were remarkably talented and devoted their lives to a wide range of intellectual pursuits. Mary was a polymath. She studied musicology, ornithology and social history. She became a reader at the Bodleian library, Oxford and was given a scholarship for research at Trinity College, Cambridge. Armitt founded a library in Ambleside which still thrives today (now also incorporating a museum and gallery) and is well worth a visit.

Grasmere author Mary Armitt

Extract from The Church of Grasmere – Mary Armitt, 1912

The parish of Grasmere also embraced three townships. One was Grasmere proper, situated in the basin-shaped vale that catches the sources of the Rothay, Langdale; the sister valley formed the second township, which extended to Elterwater; the third was Rydal-and-Loughrigg (often called Loughrigg and Beneath-Moss) which included all the rocky mass between the converging rivers, the compact village of Rydal with part of Ambleside.

From three sides of the parish then, by mountain path and 'horse-trod', the folk wended their way for worship to Grasmere church. Those of the vale of Grasmere proper would gather in units or little groups from all the scattered farmsteads, from Far Easdale and Blindtarn Gill, from Town Head, Gill Side, and all the houses that lay 'Aboon Beck' as far as How Head and Town End, till they met at their lych-gate on the north side of the church.
From Loughrigg and Beneath-Moss they would collect by many a devious track starting from as far back as Clappersgate and Ambleside. From Ambleside ancient 'trods' passed Nook End, and rose from Scandale Bridge by easy grade to Nab Lane (where Rydal folk would join them) and White Moss, and thence descending to cross the church bridge to enter the garth by the present gate, which was specially their own.

The third stream of worshippers flowed from the farthest source west, from the recesses of Little Langdale, from Blea Tarn, and Fell Foot, from Forge and Hackett and Colwith they came, on through Elterwater, and across Walthwaite Bottom. Mounting the brow, they would meet a tributary stream of fellow-townsfolk, that gathered right from Steel End and Wall End, increasing as it flowed down Mickle Langdale, till it crossed the ridge of Hunting Stile. Dropping steeply into the vale, they would at Nichols (where stood an inn) meet a third contingent (from Loughrigg) which, starting at Skelwith, mounted by Foul Step to Little Loughrigg, passed by the Fold, the Oaks and Scroggs, to descend by Red Bank to the level of Grasmere Lake.*

From Nichols onward the united groups would travel by the lake, and past the Holy Well, to enter the church garth by a gate at the north-west angle, now gone, called the Langdale gate **.

Here, at Church Stile, stood an important inn, long owned by the Harrison family. Shelter and a fire must indeed have been often needed (as well as something for the inner man) after the long travel – especially at funeral gatherings, when the corpse had to be borne through ford and flood, or through the storms and deep snows of winter time. The Ambleside folk, when in 1674 they petitioned their bishop for the right of burial in their chapel, stated that "by reason of the heat in summer and the great snowes and sudden inundations of water in winter it is very difficult and dangerous to carry their dead thither (to Grasmere) for burial"; yet their distance from the church was nothing like that of the Langdale folk. There were not infrequent burials from the right bank of Little Langdale beck, in the parish of Hawkshead or of 'Ulverston'.

Once within the churchyard, the different streams of the townships mingled as fellow parishioners. The sexes, however, divided, the women seeking entrance (presumably) by the great south porch, and the men (after business done) herding in the west door, known as theirs. Yet once inside, they again fell rigorously into ranks of townships, as we shall see.

A rushbearing tradition is still continued at Grasmere

* There is a tradition that a route from Skelwith Bridge dropped sharply from the top of Red Bank to the old ford of the Rothay known as Bathwath (Rydal Hall, MSS), and that it had even been used for funerals. This seems unlikely, unless the use were a repetition of a custom that had prevailed before the present Red Bank road was made; and of superstitious adherence to old corpse-roads the Rev J C Atkinson (*Forty Years in a Moorland Parish*) gives instances. There may indeed have been once a well-trodden path there. In former times a fulling-mill stood on the left bank of the Rothay, near to the ford, and within the freehold property of Bainrigg. The mill was owned by the Benson family in the fifteenth century, but Bainrigg had belonged before that time to a family of de Bainbrigg, who had at least one capital dwelling or mansion-house

'The most loveliest spot that man hath ever found'

— William Wordsworth's description of Rydal Mount, near Grasmere

standing upon it. Now a road to this house or houses there must have been. The woodman recently found a track leading up from the site of the mill to the rocky height, which emerged upon the present Wishing-Gate road. On the line of this (which was engineered as a turnpike road only about 1770-80) the older way doubtless continued towards Grasmere, past How Top and through Town End. A huge stone standing on the line was known as the How Stone. Levi Hodgson who lived at How Top, and who described the route to Mr W H Hills remembered fragments of a cottage in the wood. If the Skelwith Bridge folk ever used it as a church path, they would meet their townsmen (who had come over White Moss) at How Top. Close by there is still a flat-topped boulder used for resting burdens upon.

** This gate is shown in a map of 1846, as well as the stile which gave its name to the house then still standing, that was immediately opposite. Both disappeared as the widening of the lane from Stock Bridge to the church.

Nab Well

The Grasmere Corpse Road attracts thousands of tourists each year but most trundle quickly past one of the iconic Wordsworthian spots without realising it. Nab Well is a spring which is just a few yards from Rydal Mount and was much loved by both William and Dorothy. He was no doubt thinking of spots like Nab Well when he described the countryside around Rydal Mount as "the loveliest spot that man hath ever found". The two of them planted flowers and ferns around the well (so were not happy when one passer-by said to them, 'What a nice well that would be if all that rubbish was cleared off' – he meant the flowers they had planted!). From 1813 until his dying day, Wordsworth drank water from the well and wrote a poem entirely devoted to the spring. But the arrival of tap water at the start of the 20th Century led to the neglect of springs like Nab Well. St Oswald's holy well to the west of Grasmere was turfed over and can no longer be found. George Middleton writing in 1918 said: "Near the middle of last century, with the object of evening the land's surface and winning a few square yards of

Nab Well – "no pitcher dips to move it to merriment"

pasture, the rude masonry about the well was removed and the cavity filled up and turfed. Thus was effaced for ever a charming picture illustrating the first phase of the dales folk's Christian life."

Middleton rejoiced that Nab Well still survived – just. "Many whose lives have been sweetened by contact with Wordsworth pass and repass Nab Well little dreaming that it was once so precious to their teacher's heart. It now presents a sad, forsaken, unrespected look; no pitcher dips to move it to merriment."

He was writing 100 years ago but could have written those words last week for they perfectly describe the precarious state of the well today. It's a pity.

Equally famous in the 19th Century was Nab Oak. Its location is uncertain and may have long since gone but this glorious oak below Nab Well must be a contender

A 19th Century illustration of Nab Well by Harry Goodwin

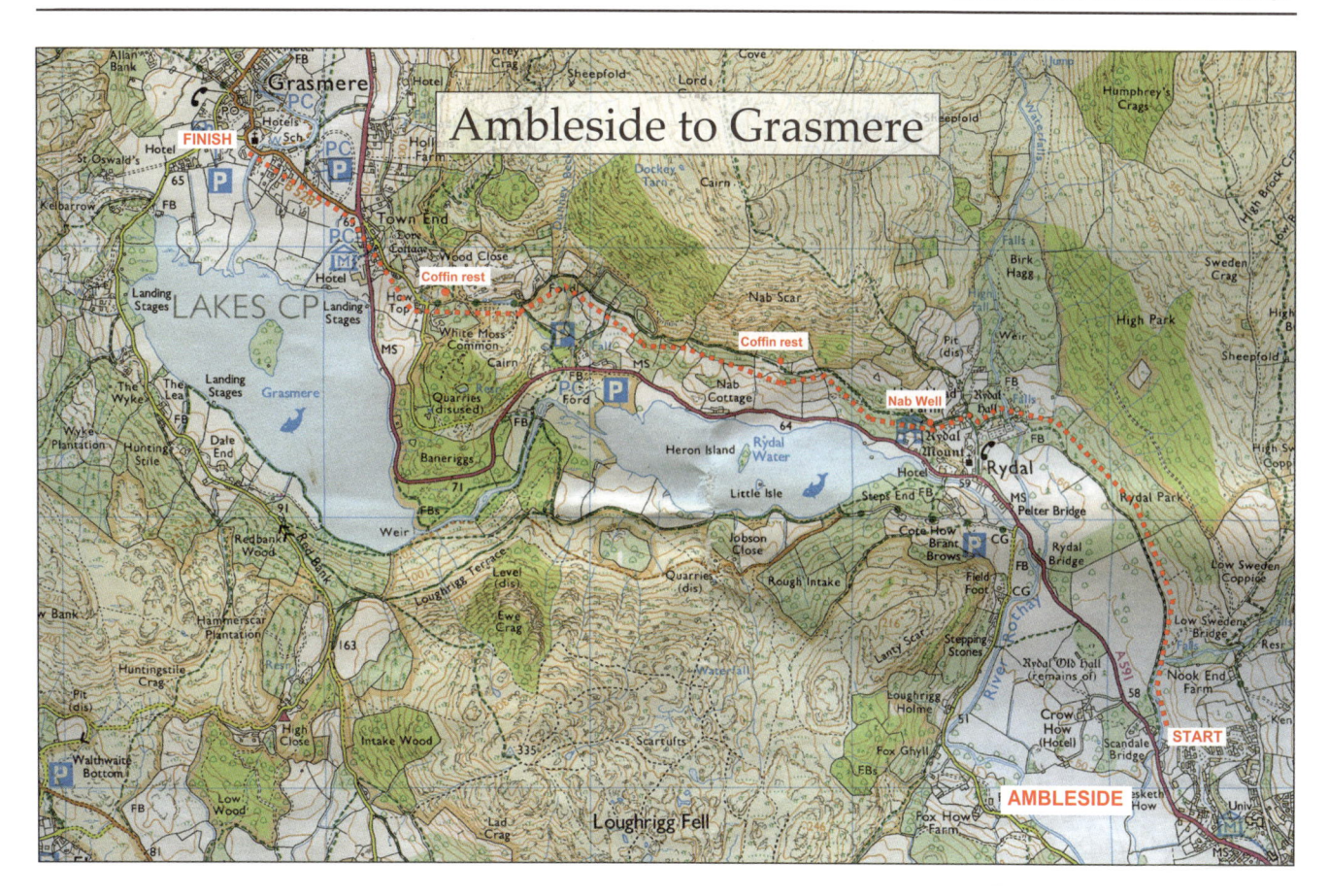

THE CORPSE ROADS OF CUMBRIA　　　　　　　　　　　　　　　　　　　AMBLESIDE TO GRASMERE : 37

Ambleside to Grasmere

The Ambleside to Grasmere Corpse Road above Rydal Mount

The Walk

Distance: 6km
Grade: Easy to medium. Ambleside to Rydal is suitable for wheelchairs. After that the path becomes increasing difficult over some rockky terrain.
Map: OL7 – Explorer
Start: The corpse road starts in Ambleside and heads to St Oswald's Church, Grasmere though it's pleasant enough to walk in either direction. Ambleside is a delightful town and you can start at St Mary's Church built in 1854. There are car parks in the town centre, including an 'honesty box' car park at the school near the church. Head out of the town on the A591 Rydal Road. As you leave the town you will pass the Armitt museum dedicated to Mary

Armitt and the history of Ambleside; well worth a visit. After about a quarter of a mile you'll see on the right hand side of the road a bus stop and a driveway leading to Rydal Hall – this is the start of the corpse road proper. Make your way towards Rydal Hall (don't worry it's a public path) and if you wish take time to enjoy the gardens. You'll also find a cafe and toilets here. The path leads out of Rydal Hall and takes you to a short road leading to Rydal Mount, the former home of the Wordsworths. Again you may wish to take time out to visit Rydal Mount. Just a few yards up the hill you'll see the corpse route signposted, heading north. The path is outlined at first by drystone walls before reaching a gate that takes you onto the fell. Just beyond this gate is the famous but neglected Nab Well. Keep an eye out for it. The path is easy to follow and you'll enjoy some grand views of Rydal Water and Grasmere. You'll also see other sights including the fallen tree trunk which tourists have hammered coins in to (no one knows why!), the coffin rest that is now a seat and plenty of wildlife. Eventually you'll drop down onto a single-track road that leads to Howe Head and turns towards Dove Cottage. You'll see the other coffin rest signposted by the road shortly before Dove Cottage. From Dove Cottage carefully cross the road into Grasmere village itself and in the centre you'll find St Oswald's Church which has the graves of the Wordsworths.

Things to See: Dove Cottage, Wordsworth Museum, St Oswald's Church, The Gingerbread Shop, Grasmere lake, Rydal caves, Rydal Mount, the Armitt Museum.

Watch for this unusual tree on the Grasmere corpse road. For no particular reason, passers-by hammer coins into it

Chapel Stile to Grasmere

A Grasmere corpse road featuring the delightful Huntingstile Lonning

'We have no book for strange preachers'

— A note in the registers of Langdale church, 1732

THE corpse road from Ambleside to Grasmere is so well known it often gets incredibly busy. But the 'other' Grasmere corpse road is usually devoid of tourists and, in our mind, a much nicer walk. It begins at Holy Trinity Church at Chapel Stile and the 4km trek over the fell to Grasmere is an easy one with breathtaking views. Further, there are cafes and pubs at both Chapel Stile and Grasmere! Holy Trinity was completed in 1858 but there had been worship on the site for several centuries. The dead had to be taken for burial to St Oswald's Church, Grasmere. Hugh Ellison in his booklet, Church and Chapel in the Langdales (1958) records the north aisle of Grasmere church came to be known as Langdale Side and "there was also a Langdale gate at one time in the north-west corner of the churchyard". Amazingly, the funeral bier used to carry the corpse from Chapel Stile to Grasmere is still held by the church (see picture on p41). In 1821, the Rev William Jackson petitioned the Bishop of Chester for permission to allow burials in the churchyard at Chapel Stile and the ground was consecrated on 3rd September 1821.

In addition to Mary Armitt's description of the corpse road, there are a number of newspaper reports from the 19th Century which make mention of it, particularly over Huntingstile Lonning. When Grasmere's churchyard became 'full up' and was closed in 1892, the *Sunderland Daily Echo* reported (5 March 1892):

Grasmere Churchyard: *The 'Churchyard among the mountains' is to be closed by an Order in Council. At one time bodies used to be brought for burial here over a path across the fells, still known as the 'corpse-road' from the neighbouring valley of Langdale; but this has been long discontinued.*

The path dropping down at Huntingstile from the fell is famous for another reason: It is featured in a delightful dialect Christmas poem, *Down't Lonnin'*, read most years at the Grasmere Christmas readings. It is sadly anonymous and we reprint it on p48 to be shared with a wider audience.

Holy Trinity Church at Chapel Stile is the proud owner of a fascinating piece of history: the funeral bier on which the dead were carried to their last resting place. It's not known for sure if this was used to take bodies to Grasmere but it would have been a practical option. Rev'd George Wrigley and Mr James Park are pictured with the bier.

42 : CHAPEL STILE TO GRASMERE	THE CORPSE ROADS OF CUMBRIA

Chapel Stile to Grasmere

Chapel Stile to Grasmere

Distance: 4km
Map: OL7 – Explorer
Grade: Fairly easy but we still recommend you take a map and compass. Those in wheelchairs can take the single-track road via High Close.
Parking: There are a few car parks in Elterwater. You'll also find cafes, toilets and pubs in Elterwater and Chapel Stile.
Things to see: We recommend calling into the church at Chapel Stile. Aside from the beauty of the villages and fells, keep an eye out for wildlife. Red squirrels frequent Huntingstile and – incredibly – we have even seen an otter in Huntingstile. The village of Grasmere includes much to see including the church, the Gingerbread shop, Dove Cottage, Allan Bank and much more.

The leper's door at St Oswald's Church, Grasmere

The walk: This is currently our favourite walk although we normally do it the other way round: from Grasmere to Chapel Stile and back. However, the corpses in medieval times would have travelled from Chapel Stile in the Langdales over the fell for burial at St Oswald's Church, Grasmere.

There are car parks at Elterwater and it is just a short walk from there to the 'Langdale parish church' at Chapel Stile. The church itself is tucked into the side of the fell and is well worth a visit with its sweet stained glass window of St Francis featuring a red squirrel – and you may be lucky enough to see a real one on your walk.

Head off south-east from the church along a well-made road. After

44 : CHAPEL STILE TO GRASMERE THE CORPSE ROADS OF CUMBRIA

The start of the walk: Chapel Stile

A stained glass squirrel at Chapel Stile

And see real ones around Huntingstile

about a quarter of a mile it meets up with the road coming up from Elterwater. Shortly after this you need to branch off north-east to head up the fell. There is a signpost but

watch out for the lone silver birch tree on the horizon (see picture p45). It is in the Huntingstile Crag gap. This is the start of the steep – but short – climb onto the fell top. It's so

enjoyable it's almost too short but after following the well-trodden path over the fell it goes through the fell gate and starts to drop down into Grasmere. You will see the lake

The lone silver birch: Head for this!

On the fell top: Past Huntingstile Crag

Nearly there: The view from Huntingstile

below you. Follow the path through another gate and there is a seat on which you can enjoy your bait (dialect for lunch!) and the view over Grasmere lake. From here you can take an alternative route and divert south-east through Redbank Wood and take the path around the lake; Mary Armitt suggests this as a possible corpse road route joining up with the Ambleside to Grasmere path. However, we recommend carrying on down the wonderful Huntingstile Lonning. This is beautiful at any time of the year but in the autumn is particularly glorious with the leaves on the ground. Keep an eye out for the red squirrels and other wildlife. Eventually you will reach the main road. Turn left and carry on into the village. You will pass the Faery tearoom en route and there are many other cafes in the village itself. Sadly the holy well that once existed by Wreay Cottage was covered over in the early part of the 20th Century. The road will take you directly to St Oswald's Church in Grasmere. Enjoy your time in the village before making your way back over the corpse road to Chapel Stile.

Journey's End: St Oswald's Church, Grasmere

Huntingstile Lonning, near Grasmere, in its autumn glory

Down't Lonnin' – Anonymous

SADLY, the authors of many of our favourite poems are unknown. Who wrote them, when and why is likely to remain a mystery. Such is the case with Down't Lonnin' (Down a Country Lane). This delightful Christmas poem was brought to my attention by Grasmere storyteller Taffy Thomas in his book, *Cumbrian Folk Tales*. He heard it from the late Joyce Withers who performed it at the annual Christmas Readings staged by Grasmere Players. It sets the Christmas story in Grasmere and incorporates a number of local place names, including the lonning/corpse road at Huntingstile.

Down t' lonnin' they came,
Just Braithwaite's Mary with Joe,
That she wed Lammas year,
And their li'le lad in her arm.

Moon was low and clear
Above Silver How, and mists writhin' up from t'lake,
And light sharp and silver, as 'tis

Of a winter dusk with the night beginning to break
On the darkening dale.
There were no mysteries
Round Mary and Joe;
They smiled at us, going by —
'Grand evening!' Joe called out, and Postie said 'Aye!'
And our Libby, she ran to set them a bit on road,
As Mary turned, and showed
T'bairn sleeping soft and warm...

Up Huntingstile they went;
And the young moon dropped over Silver How
And the night shut down; and now
We saw them no more;
    their footsteps after a while
Died into mists and darkness.

Up lonnin' they came
Late in the evenin';
We never heard them come,
Though night was still
As a sheltered tarn is — only a whisper from

The li'le beck near at hand,
    splashin' down in spate.
Quiet they came, and late,
And none said owt as they passed us — just so
A young lass, walking wearily, and a man
 ... like Joe ... Or not so like, maybe?
... and the two of 'em bent
Over a bairn asleep; and as they went
Through the dark trees and lake mists,
    there was light.

Up lonnin' they came,
Just Braithwaite's lass wi' her man,
On a winter's night —
Just Braithwaite's Mary — who else?

Loweswater

An easy ramble with grand views and a famous Inn at journey's end

'A love of the fells, a desire to escape from the common round, a long-standing interest in maps and an acquired interest in drawing... and an insatiable urge to look round the next corner on a trodden way'

— **Alfred Wainwright**

THE National Trust and other websites have promoted a path running through High Nook Farm and skirting under Burnbank Fell as the Loweswater Corpse Road. However, we are grateful to Dr Roger Asquith, a retired research engineer with an interest in local history, for discovering this is an error and the path through Holme Wood is almost certainly the true corpse road. He points out the Loweswater Enclosure map shows the higher path, in 1865/6, whereas the first edition of the Ordnance Survey map (OS1) of 1863/4 did not show it. Hence we know the age of the path to within a year or so. This higher road therefore dates back just over 150 years — some way short of the corpse road era over 600 years ago. Indeed, Dr Asquith also notes that the vicar of Loweswater in 1929 — J Rowland

– wrote of "the tradition, which still exists in the parish… the dead from Loweswater used to be carried via the 'corpse road' *through* Holmwood, for burial at St Bees" (*A Few Notes on the Church & Parish*).

Dr Asquith adds: "The Maggies Lonning - Watergate - Hudson Place - Jenkinson Place - Iredale Place - Fangs path shown on the OS1 (surveyed in 1863/4) was the ancient way on the south side of the lake, linking the habitations before heading off towards Lamplugh. Clear from the maps and on the ground is the fact that this ancient track was well made, well defined and important. Until modern times it had a wall on either side before emerging onto and crossing the common to join the Fangs to Lamplugh road."

The Loweswater corpse road through Holme Wood

Research by Derek Denman indicates parochial status was granted to Loweswater in 1403 and 'the dead have not been carried to St Bees for over 600 years'. Dr Asquith adds: "What was formerly The Holme, now Holme Wood, was finally enclosed after much dispute, in about 1597 so, at the time of the corpse road, beyond Watergate lay open common."

We're grateful to Dr Asquith for 'restoring' the correct corpse road route and there's an extra advantage: For the most part the corpse road through Holme Wood is a well-made wheelchair-friendly path making it accessible to many more people. It's only as it climbs towards Fangs Brow that that path gets tougher. The higher path may have been incorrectly promoted as a corpse road but it is nonetheless a path that offers breath-taking views of the fells and you may wish to use it to make your return journey for a different perspective of Loweswater.

Shortly after leaving St Bartholomew's Church, the corpse road drops down into the valley through Maggie's Lonning. 'Lonning' is a dialect term for 'lane' and most of the lonnings surviving in the county are still only footpaths.

Loweswater's famous 'shy' signpost: It tells you where you can't go, but not where you can.

Maggie's Lonning is now a tarmacked road but has not lost all of its character. It is a single track road (NY 136 210) that leads to the impossibly-small car park by Loweswater. We suggest only trying to use this car park midweek in the middle of winter. It quickly gets full-up and there is almost nowhere to turn round once you are stuck in the traffic jam. It's a Lake District feature that needs a serious rethink. There is not much parking elsewhere in the valley so we recommend parking in one of the lay-bys beside the lake or by the side of the road at Fangs Brow (and therefore do the corpse road in reverse). Since the corpse road is essentially one half of a round-the-lake walk it does not matter too much where you start.

This is a lovely walk but there's not much history or legend to go with it. However author HC Ivison includes an intriguing entry in her book, *Supernatural Cumbria* (2010) about a ghostly funereal procession apparently witnessed by the lake: *"The apparitions of three nuns carrying what appeared to be a shrouded corpse, was a reported unexplained event that made the national newspapers. It was in the early 1920s, and four young ex-soldiers were walking along by Loweswater Lake in the moonlight, when they witnessed this sight. In spite of later ridicule, they held to their story and the fact that they were sober. Frank Carruthers comments that local records attest to an apparently similar apparition being seen by several witnesses some 21 years before, which would make it around the turn of the 19th and 20th Century. There is as far as my present knowledge goes, neither explanation, or any story or legend that might possibly account for these events. Local folklore does talk of monks and a monastery in Loweswater Valley but thus far no mention of nuns."*

The wonderful view over Loweswater

It's a fascinating and suggestive tale but we have been unable to find the report in any newspapers or any mention in the works of Frank Carruthers.

54 : LOWESWATER — THE CORPSE ROADS OF CUMBRIA

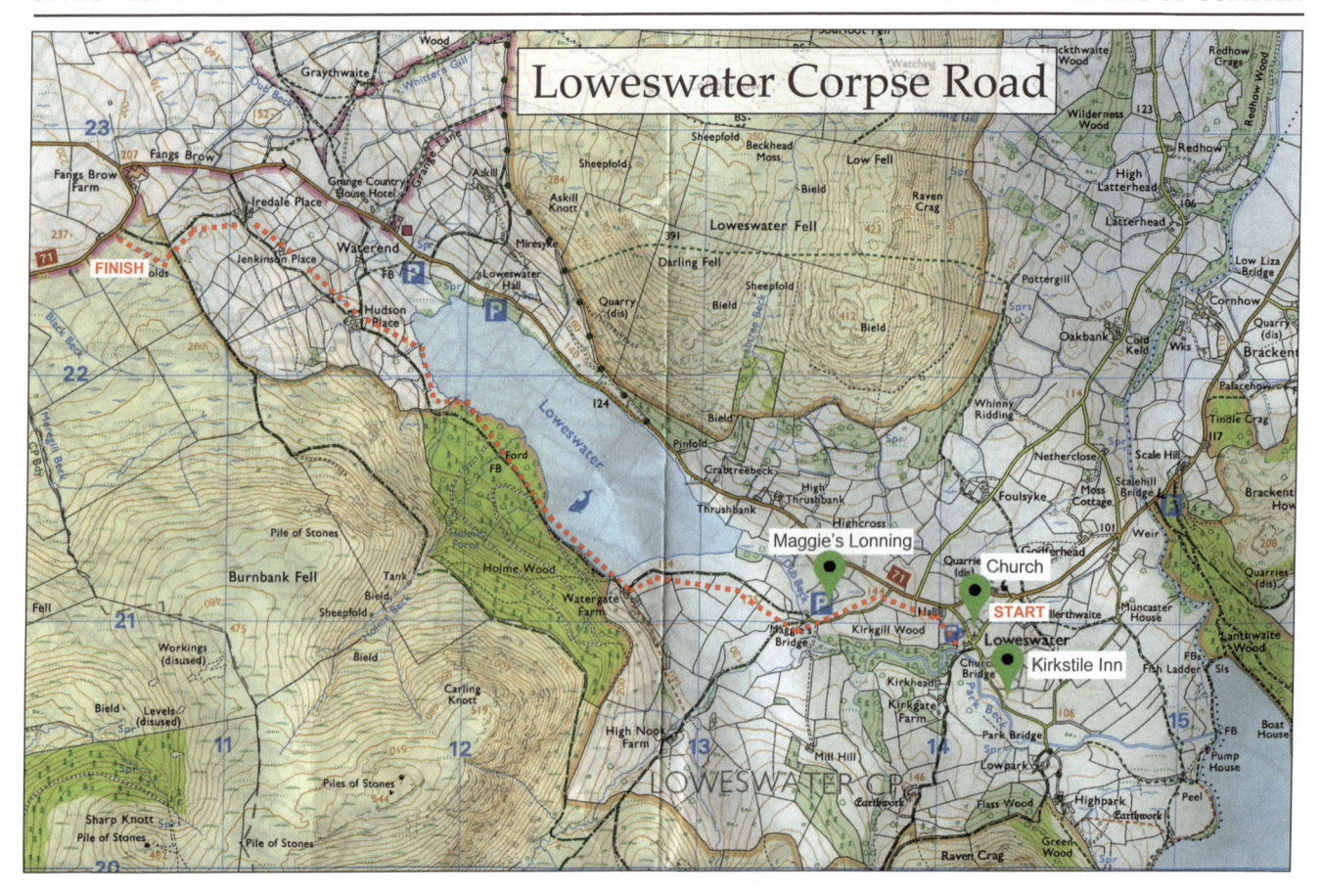

Loweswater

Distance: About 6km

Grade: Easy access for wheelchair users or those with limited mobility as far as Holme Wood.

Map: OL4 – Explorer

Start: There is a public car park at the end of Maggie's Lonning but this is small and it might be better to park in one of the lay-bys by the lake.

The Route: You can start anywhere as you can include the corpse road as a circular route around the lake. However, the 'official' start would be at St Bartholomew's Church (originally a chapel of ease) and then heading in the direction of Lamplugh and St Bees. Drop down to the lake through Maggie's Lonning and you'll then take the path through the car park and towards the lake. This is a good path and suitable for people in wheelchairs or limited mobility. The path stays good even through Holme Wood but becomes more difficult as you climb out of the wood and through Hudson Place, Jenkinson Place and Iredale Place. You'll end at Fangs Brow and you can then come back via the fellside path and High Nook Farm or the other side of the lake.

Refreshments: The Kirkstile Inn is the famed eating place in this valley (we've marked its location on the map).

St Bartholomew's Church, Loweswater

Maggie's Lonning

Who was Maggie and why was the lonning named after her? There's also a packhorse bridge nearby called Maggie's Bridge (even OS mark it as such) so she appears to have been at one time a famous or well-loved person in the valley. We were unable to find out until recently and it was thanks to the work of the British Newspaper Archives project which is slowly but surely scanning 400 years of newspaper archives into digital format, making them easily accessible and, more importantly, searchable. During a search I found a note about Maggie's Lonning at Loweswater. It was in *The Cumberland Pacquet* for 1833:

Maggie's Lonning, Loweswater

"VILLAGE FAME – A clever and worthy old lady, sister to the eldest of the three venerable men named in the preceding paragraph (ie John Mirehouse, of Miresike, who died aged 102) and who died at the good old age of 98 years, although never the owner of a foot of land has had the honour of having her name perpetuated in her native vale (Loweswater) in Maggie's Lonning (lane or road), Maggie's Bridge, Maggie's Gate, Maggie's House, Maggie's Garden and her 'flowers grown wild' and even the very birds in Maggie's Robin and various anecdotes of Maggie's sayings and doings. Poor Maggie! her garden no longer smiles, and her house now lies in ruins."

The preceding paragraph talked about the Mirehouse family which "furnishes such instances of longevity as are rarely to be met with". In particular it spoke of Maggie's brother, John Mirehouse, who died in 1807 at the age of 102. A further Google search revealed that *The Literary Panorama* (Published 1808) told how on his 100th birthday he "received a very numerous party of his neighbours ('all his juniors') seated in a new oak chair, and cloathed in a new coat, which, he pleasantly observed, might, with care taken, serve his life-time." But what more of Maggie? The tantalising paragraph indicates she was indeed well loved and something of a village character but sadly not much more. Further historic research revealed she had been born on St Valentine's Day 1714 in Loweswater and later married to become Margaret Longmire. She died in her 93rd year (ie 1807) on Tuesday, July 14th at Thrushbank, Loweswater. But the *Pacquet* said she lived to be 98. Further research may resolve that mystery although the burial records kindly put online by the Lorton & Derwent Fells Local History Society do not include her.

So for now, we can at least revive the identity of Maggie as Maggie Longmire (nee Mirehouse) who was born on February 14th, 1714 and died in 1807 or 1813. And at least we still have her lonning – and bridge.

Further Reading

Loweswater Church Guide by AK Ames and DA Edwards
Supernatural Cumbria by HC Ivison. Amberley, 2010
Life In Old Loweswater by Roz Southey

Websites
British Newspaper Archive:
www.britishnewspaperarchive.co.uk
Lorton & Derwent Fells Local History Society: www.derwentfells.com
Lakes Guides: www.lakesguides.co.uk

Irton

The 'spaghetti junction' of Cumbrian corpse roads

"I call the living
I toll for the dead
And stop the lightning"

– the inscription on one of the bells at St Paul's references the belief that ringing a bell could drive away thunderstorms

FOR the most part corpse roads are more myth than fact; vague paths shrouded in the fog of time and walked only by ghosts. And yet we will see that the Irton corpse roads were dragged kicking and screaming into the harsh bright light of the courtroom and in that crucible measured, defined and ruled upon. They were found to be genuine, proven-in-law routes not to be meddled with even by the lord of the manor. Here are gold standard corpse roads, utterly beyond dispute.

The pedigree for these roads is down to a bitter row that broke out in 1899 when Thomas Brocklebank, the then owner of Irton Hall, closed off a footpath going past the windows of his manor. Local resident Joseph Burrough objected – believing this

THE CORPSE ROADS OF CUMBRIA

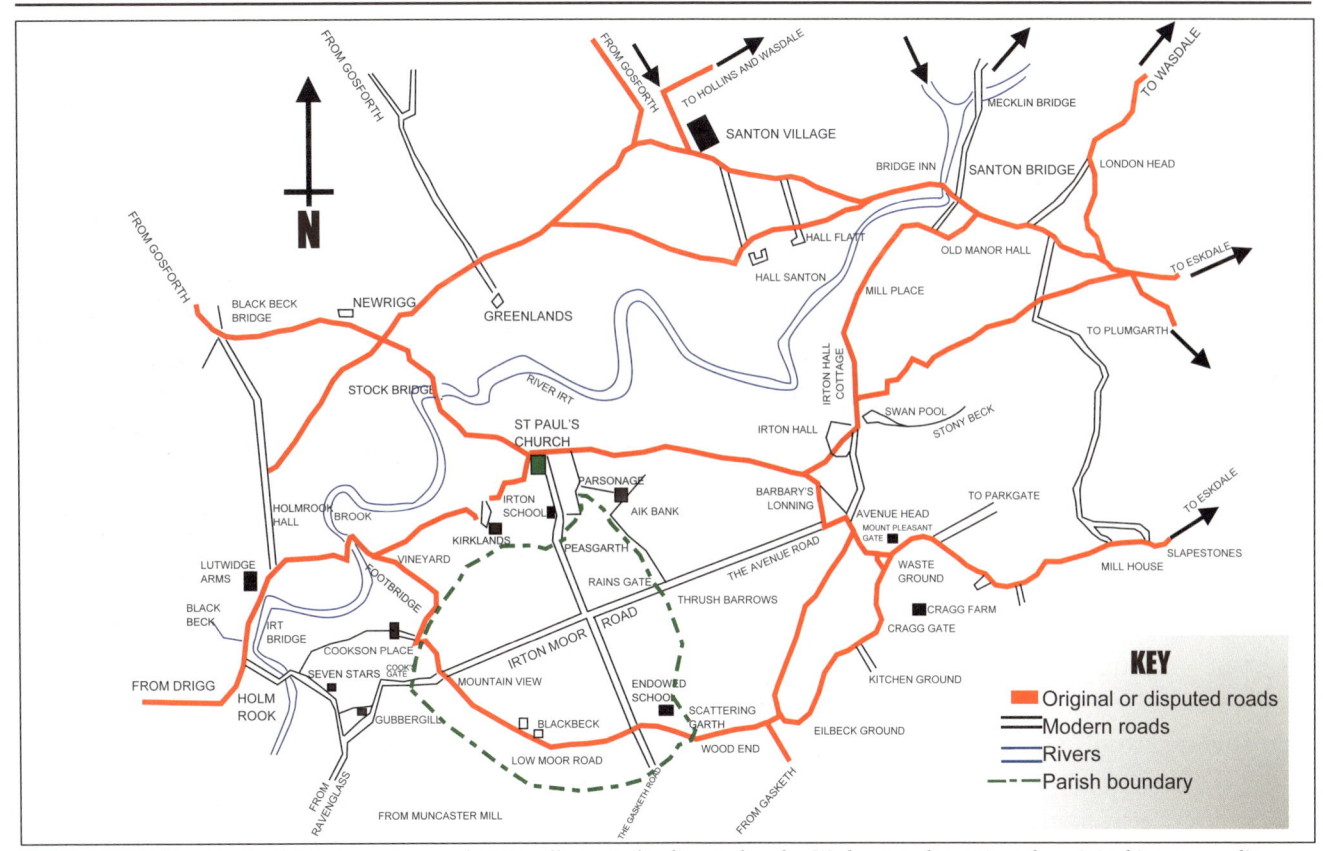

IRTON : 59

The map reproduced in the Whitehaven News of 1899 to illustrate the disputed paths. We have re-drawn it as the original is poor quality

was a right of way and had been for many centuries. He won the support of Bootle Parish Council who decided to take this fight to court. What followed was a five-year legal dispute involving dozens of witnesses that became a national *cause célèbre*. Its national notoriety centred on two things: the great time and huge cost (tens of thousands of pounds in today's money) being spent on something as 'trivial' as a footpath dispute. In fact, we'd venture to suggest this path can lay claim to being the most expensive path in Cumbria. The other aspect that caught the attention of the UK reading public was the mention in court of corpse roads and accompanying superstition. Here was medieval folklore appearing in a court case on the eve of the 20th

St Paul's Church, Irton: The focus of a network of corpse roads

Century. The local importance of the case is demonstrated by the verbatim account published in *The Whitehaven News*. It is literally word for word and we must send up a prayer of thanks to the unnamed reporter with seemingly impeccable shorthand who sat day-in, day-out in the Cumberland Assizes at Carlisle recording every cough, splutter and occasional '(laughter)'. For two weeks other news was reduced to just a few paragraphs and page after page was devoted to 'The Irton Footpath Case'.

And – a cutting-edge innovation for 1899 – they included a graphic, a map of the disputed paths. We have republished it here (p59) but, as the original is hard to read, have re-drawn it.

Irton Hall: Today a more friendly welcome awaits ramblers looking for somewhere to eat or stay

The case started on 26 January 1899 at the Cumberland Assizes in Carlisle with Mr Justice Day the judge overseeing the case. The plaintiffs were Joseph Burrough and Bootle Parish Council 'on behalf of all the other tenants of the manor of Irton and Santon. The defendants were Thomas Brocklebank of Irton Hall and his father, Sir Thomas Brocklebank, of nearby Greenland. The barrister for Burrough and Bootle was Mr Shee QC & others and for the Brocklebanks it was Sir

Edward Clarke QC MP & others. Let battle commence.

The proceedings opened with Mr Shee explaining to the judge and jury which paths were in dispute. Although the main path of contention was the one passing literally beneath the window of Irton Hall, it also took in other paths:

"The paths in dispute run from the direction of Gosforth over Blackbeck Bridge and Stockbridge past St Paul's Church, branching left and right about Irton Hall; from Holmrook Hall to the path first named; and from Holmwood to Cook's Gate."

And Mr Shee explained to the jury that, under the Local Government Act, Bootle Parish Council had a duty "to protect public rights of way" and to "prevent as soon as possible the stopping or obstruction of any such rights of way in their district". Hence the action. The paths were clearly shown on the 1860 Ordnance Survey Map and Mr Slee also pointed to their antiquity suggesting they were packhorse ways in the recent past linking Kendal and Ambleside to Seascale and Whitehaven. And he told the court he thought that in all probability they had also been used as 'cart roads'.

Ancient deeds were gone into and in 1712 the path at Vineyard (then called Ellerclose) had cropped up in a dispute and was referred to as a 'church road' (ie going to St Paul's at Irton).

Where it all began: This was the gateway closed off in 1899 which sparked the lengthy court case. It was seemingly bricked up in the 20th Century – presumably without much protest this time. It is just down the road from the entrance to Irton Hall (on the way to Santon Bridge)

The deed said: "Also we find that Wm Gaitskell (Gubberghyll), Wm Tumban (Moor End), Henry Hodgin, and Richard Walker (Cookson Place) complained against Susan Smith for not making their church road sufficient through her ground. We find Susan Smith to make their church way sufficient for bride and corpse for horse and foot betwixt and Michaelmas next, or else to be amerced in 13s 4d." The ancient custom was for people to look after and clean the stretch of public road in front of their house; it is one that austerity Britain might like to revive. A month later and the 18th Century dispute was still rumbling on: "Whereas a church way through Ellerclose ground has been in dispute, the last court before this betwixt Susan Smith on the one part and all those that claim any churchway through Ellerclose grounds, and the jury did find that the tenants or occupiers of Ellerclose should make the churchway sufficient both for horse and foot; and likewise it has been agreed by all parties concerned about said churchway to put it to the jury above mentioned where the churchway should be taken

Ellerclose: Now called The Vineyard. The corpse road runs past the house

The Irton Oak and the ghost of Lady Ann Lamplugh

In the grounds of Irton Hall stands a remarkable oak tree (see picture on p66) and it's clear that it has graced that spot for hundreds of years. With such an age to it, there can be no surprise that the Irton Oak – or King's Oak as it is also known – has at least two legends associated with it.

The best-known one tells how King Henry VI made his way to Irton after the Battle of Hexham in 1464 – a decisive Yorkist victory in the War of the Roses (a fight for the throne between the House of York symbolised by a white rose and the House of Lancaster symbolised by a red rose). Henry was on the losing Lancaster side and fled from the battlefield. Legend tells he arrived at Irton Hall and pleaded with John Irton for sanctuary. He was refused and was forced to spend the night hiding from his enemies in the oak tree. John Irton's wife – Ann Lamplugh – was apparently more sympathetic and took food to the King. Her furious husband locked Ann in the pele tower at Irton Hall as punishment and it is said her ghost still walks.

Another tale told about the tree is referred to by historian Dr CA Parker in his 1926 work, *The Gosforth District* and tells how a person once went missing. Eventually his cries were heard coming from the oak tree: He had fallen into the hollow trunk. Make sure you don't suffer a similar fate!

It was usual for notable trees and landmarks to be used to mark boundaries or key routes in the medieval landscape so it's possible this is why a path first arose here.

to make the way sufficient, we the jury above mentioned do find that the tenants or occupiers of Ellerclose ground shall make a sufficient stile, 3 foot betwixt sides, and to stand where it used to stand formerly at west end of house, for foot people to go over, and to let four foot of ground to lay untilled from the hedge for people to go over and the tenants or occupiers of Ellerclose shall find a sufficient gate at the road end of Ellerclose for horse people to go in at, and to make the way sufficient. And we find that if any of the parties shall break or resist this order, shall be amerced (fined) in 13s 4d the party aggrieved giving the defendant ten days' notice to mend the way."

What's also interesting in this account is the very specific measurements

'We the jury above mentioned do find that the tenants or occupiers of Ellerclose ground shall make a sufficient stile, 3 foot betwixt sides, and to stand where it used to stand formerly at west end of house'

detailed for the width of the path, something that became a guiding principle in footpath disputes in the future. However, the case at Carlisle Assizes was just getting started.

Mr Shee, over the next two weeks, brought forth witness after witness who recounted how they had walked the path without objection or obstruction for their whole life. In a rebuttal, Mr Clarke produced other witnesses who said they had been told by Thomas Brocklebank that the path was private.

For two weeks the jury listened to the arguments in a trial costing thousands of pounds and were then asked to deliver their verdict. They were unable to reach one; they suggested instead that the warring parties sort it out between themselves! The national papers shared the undoubted exasperation of all the parties concerned. *The Aberdeen Evening Express* for example said: "Although it will, after such a stubborn fight, go against the grain to do so, the best policy in the circumstances for the litigants is undoubtedly to follow the course recommended by both judge and jury and make an effort to come to an amicable arrangement, thus

Irton Oak: It's probably no coincidence that this ancient tree stands beside the corpse road that goes through the grounds of Irton Hall

avoiding a retrial and the throwing away of good money after bad."

The Lancashire Evening Post (March 10th, 1899) explained to readers the quaint corpse road traditions of Cumberland and in particular one aspect which had been thrashed out in court – the idea that once a path had been used to carry a coffin it was for always a public right of way:–

THE BELIEF IN 'CORPSE ROADS'

The trial, after lasting a fortnight, although nominally for a much greater principle, was, says a contemporary, *to a certain extent practically to determine the existence today of privileges believed to be conferred by a very old custom. Most of the witnesses for the defence had something to say about the path chiefly in dispute being a 'church path' or a 'corpse road'. Into the merits of the dispute it is not necessary to enter; the aspect now mentioned is simply one of antiquarian interest. It recalls the days when hearses were unknown; when the coffin was carried shoulder high by relays of men – often by the sons or other male relatives of the deceased – to the church, taking scrupulous care to travel by the corpse road. To the present time these routes are carefully followed, and the belief has not yet died that serious results to land-owners might follow a deviation, the passing of a corpse over a road making it a public thoroughfare. In north Cumberland it was a general belief that on the death of any person, his spirit, with the form and colour of a faint flame, passed along the 'burial road' to the church and up to where the coffin would rest. thence it was believed to go to the grave, where in the case of a good man, it sometimes allowed itself to be seen again.*

FROM THE IRTON COURT ROLLS

Under the date 1st January 1712 there was the following entry in the rolls:

"Also we find that Wm Gaitskell (Gubberghyll), Wm Tumban (Moor End), Henry Hodgin, and Richard Walker (Cookson Place) complained against Susan Smith for not making their church road sufficient through her ground. We find Susan Smith to make their church way sufficient for bride and corpse for horse and foot betwixt and Michaelmas next, or else to be amerced (fined) in 13s 4d."

See separate section on bridal paths on p70.

The jury at Carlisle, having failed to reach a verdict, suggested instead (backed by the judge) that the parties just sit down and sort things out for themselves rather than relying on the courts. But it seems too much bad blood had already been spilt and the legal action continued for another four years. It finally ended in the Chancery Division of the High Court. The villagers won. Mr Justice Joyce found "the path had been used as a right for as long back as living memory extended".

The trial had cost tens of thousands of pounds and had become a national talking point. But at last the people of Irton had won. So what of the paths today? Well they still survive as public paths but some are not in a good state. The original path past Irton Hall's window has now been moved to the driveway. This seemed such an obvious solution to the problem at the time but it seems the people of Irton wanted their original path and weren't going to allow the Lord of the Manor to close it off.

Much work has been done of late to repair and maintain this corpse road and we hope this book continues to encourage people to walk the path. The walks we suggest take in just some of the corpse roads. Irton Hall is now open to visitors requiring refreshment, Woodland's tea room is nearby and there are a number of pubs and other refreshment places. And of course the church has its magnificent Burne-Jones windows.

February 28, 1903: A verdict at last

Further down the hill from Irton Hall and on the opposite side of the road is this curious gateway which, it is said locally, is the continuation of the church path. It fizzles out today but would originally have continued into the Eskdale valley

Path problems

In England and Wales it's the responsibility of local councils to make sure paths and access land are open and easy for walkers to use. The body responsible for maintaining public rights of way and keeping them free from obstruction is called the Highway Authority. In practice, this is the county council or unitary authority. In Scotland, the legal situation is different, as walkers enjoy a right to roam on most land. You can report problems to the council or via the website of The Ramblers organisation at www.ramblers.org.uk

Bridal paths

Bridal – *adjective – of a woman about to be married, or of a marriage ceremony*

Bridle – *noun – a set of leather straps that are put around a horse's head to allow its rider to control it.*

Bridle path – *a track in the countryside that you ride horses on*

– Cambridge dictionary

The corpse road sometimes doubled as a bridal path for weddings

THE 'grammar geeks' love to point out when someone has used the wrong spelling of bridal. It crops up mostly when someone writes about a 'bridal path' when they mean 'bridle path'. "It's to do with riding horses on a path, not to do with a young wife," they cry out. But it's not that clear cut. The further you go back in time, the more the two spellings get confused and there were indeed bridal paths to the church – referring to a path for the bride. The Irton Footpath case talked about corpse roads and about bridal paths and they meant the path by which the bride travelled to church for her wedding. And just to add to the confusion, she may well have gone there on horseback – making it a bridle path and a bridal path! Did the original bridal path become mis-spelt to give us bridle path? Probably but we may never know for sure.

It was the custom of some parts of Cumberland and Westmorland for the bride and groom to join in a race on horseback to or from the church sometimes with a prize of garters or a silk handkerchief. Here, for example, is a letter written in 1821 by Dora Harcourt in which she describes a Christmas Day wedding held near Whitehaven:

"Picture to yourself a motley assemblage of men and women all mounted on horses of every description, racing in the utmost confusion at the fastest speed towards the church. An elderly spinster reached it first, and very proud she seemed. I could scarcely believe this was really the expected wedding party, nor that they had ridden thus, starting from the bride's house, at least six miles. My aunt said they were indebted to the frost, which had rendered riding at all anything but safe, for their unusual exemption from the mud, which generally bespatters alike both men and women on each occasions."

Some European churches had doors specifically designated as 'bridal doors' which would be used for marriages – just as they also had the 'devil's door' for use at funerals.

Further reading:

The Letters of Dora Harcourt – concerning the customs and traditions of Whitehaven in 1820. With notes by Alan Cleaver. Available on Amazon.

The Folklore of the Lake District – Marjorie Rowling, 1976

Walking for Softies – Lynn Pattison. Includes many walks around Irton

The Irton corpse road leading down to the River Irt from Greenlands

Irton Walk One: Irton Hall to St Paul's Church

Prepare to enjoy a walk along the most expensive footpath in Britain! The 1899-1903 legal dispute involving dozens of witnesses may have confirmed this path as a public right of way but it also cost a small fortune in legal fees. Perhaps the only positive to off-set the huge cost of this case was the notoriety and national outcry helped lead to today's cheaper system of having inspectors rather than judges decide footpath disputes.

GRADE: The path can get muddy but is otherwise quite easy to do.

Start: The entrance to Irton Hall

DISTANCE: 1.5km. It should take about 30 minutes there and 30 minutes back
MAP: OL6 – Explorer
THE WALK: Irton Hall can be found on the Santon Bridge to Holmrook road. From Santon

A couple of hundred yards further on turn left at this signpost

Bridge, take the path past Woodland's tea rooms; Irton Hall is a few hundred yards further down. Head into the Hall's grounds and take the left-hand path/driveway until you reach a small drive off to the left (see picture top right).

Straight on: As the drive turns, go straight on

Head to the top right after the stile

The path drops down towards Aikbank field

Follow this path for a few yards and it narrows until it comes to a kissing gate. There are sheep and other animals in these fields so please keep your dog on a lead. You need to head roughly in a "2 o'clock" direction (I am saying this only for those who don't have a map and compass or aren't aware of how to take a bearing). In the far corner of the field you will see a gate with a couple of very impressive stone pillars either side. I can only assume these are relics of some former and more permanent gateway. The path drops down through a short lane which is well used by farm traffic and is therefore often quite muddy. As the ground starts to rise up you will enter an open (Aikbank) field. Again there may be cattle in this field. You are

Walk beside the wood

Finally cross the field, staying close to the fence to take you to Irton Church

heading for the far side where the wood starts. Don't go down the farm track – the gate you need is to the right of that. As you approach the gate you will see the reassuring sight of St Paul's Church, Irton in the distance. The path is at the top of a steep bank with the wood on your right and a barbed wire fence on your left. A couple more gates and you reach the church which is always open to visitors. At the rear of the church you will find the famed Irton Cross (the cross in front of the church is the war memorial), while inside are the Burne-Jones stained glass windows and many other historical features. Enjoy your visit but keep the door shut behind you to stop birds getting in.

76 : IRTON

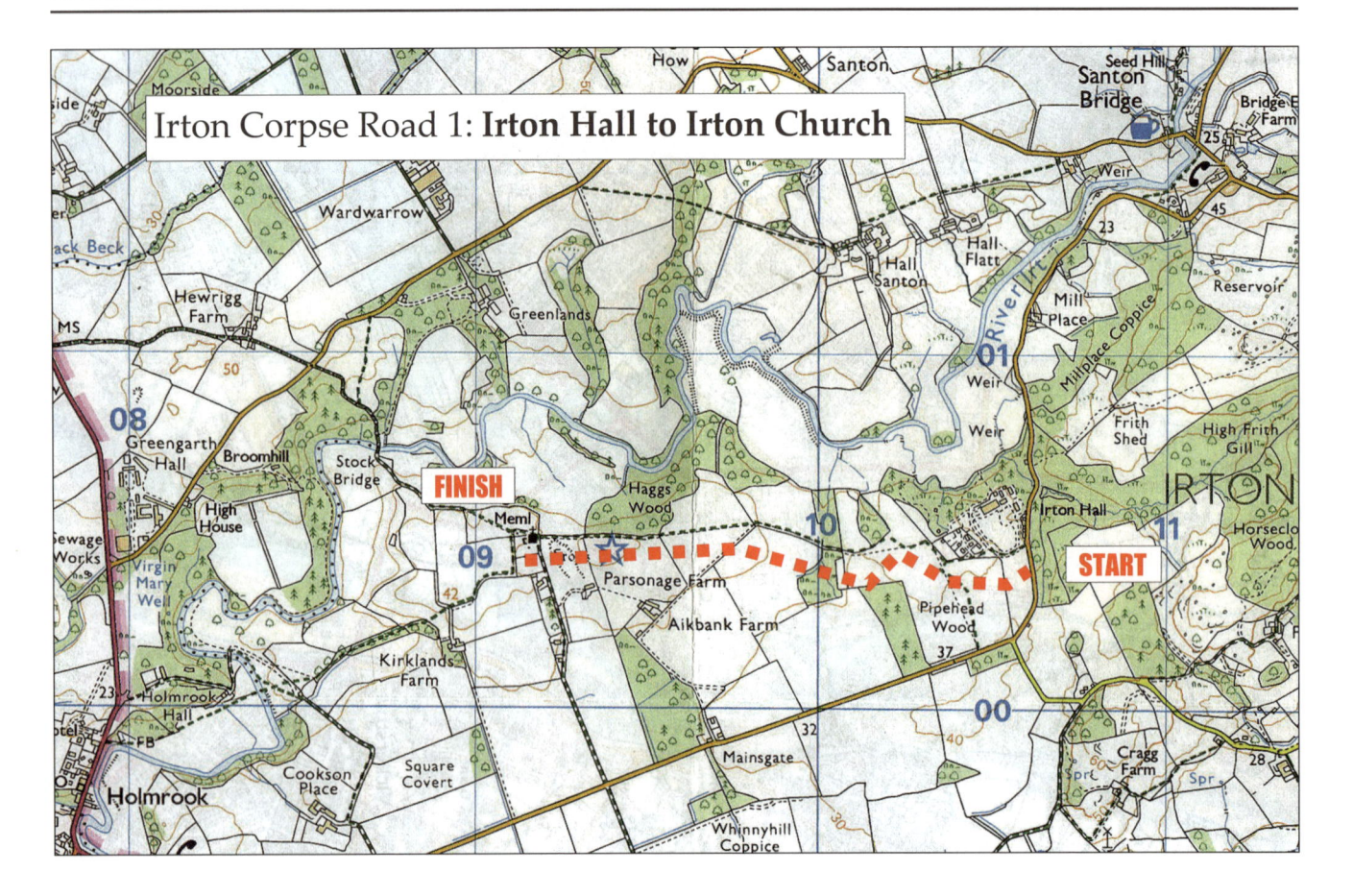

THE CORPSE ROADS OF CUMBRIA

Irton Corpse Road 1: Irton Hall to Irton Church

Burne-Jones windows

In addition to the famous Celtic Cross that stands in the churchyard, St Paul's Church at Irton can also boast four stained glass windows designed by Sir Edward Burne-Jones. The stained glass was installed during the rebuilding of the church in 1887 (to commemorate Queen Victoria's Golden Jubilee) and were a gift from Sir Thomas Brocklebank and Mr Lutwidge of Holmrook Hall. Burne-Jones (1833-1898) was closely associated with the Pre-Raphaelite movement and the windows were made by William Morris & Co. The windows show St Paul, the Tiburtine Sybil and (pictured right) St Agnes with a lamb and St Catherine of Alexandria.

78 : IRTON THE CORPSE ROADS OF CUMBRIA

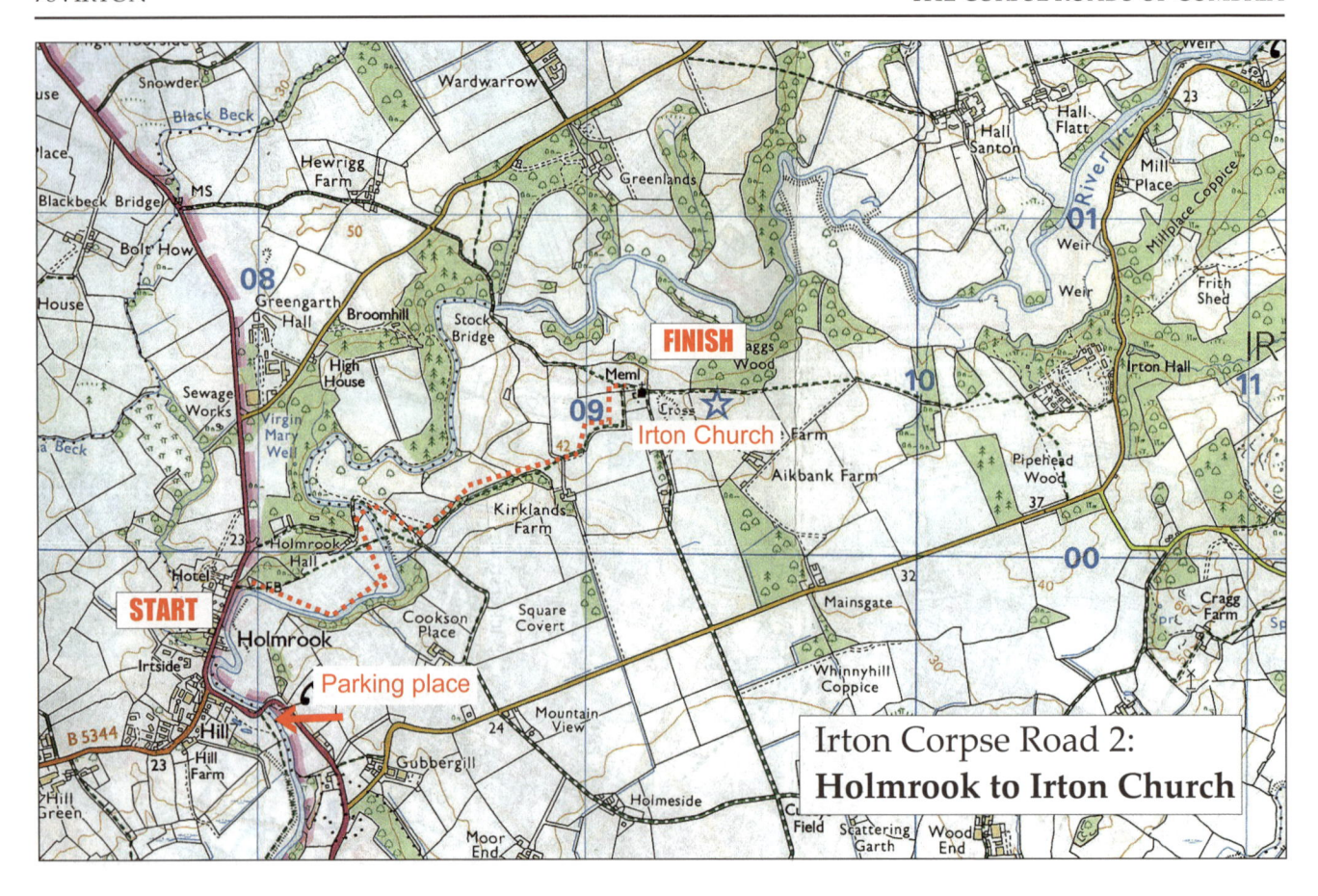

Irton Corpse Road 2:
Holmrook to Irton Church

Holmrook to Irton

THIS is the second in our Irton footpath walks and takes you from the riverside community of Holmrook up hill to St Paul's Church, Irton.

DISTANCE: About 2km

MAP: OL6 – Explorer

GRADE: Slightly difficult owing to poorly kept paths, bad signage, number of stiles and the fact that it is uphill. But don't let that put you off walking this important path.

THE WALK: Parking is probably safest in the lay-by just before the garage on the A595; then walk back

Making tracks: The start of the walk from Holmrook

to the river. You can take one of two paths from the A595 towards Irton church – the nicest one is the one that takes you by the river. But on the way back you can take the other path (it shoots off from the sharp bend just as you enter Holmrook from Gosforth) past what was once Holmrook Hall. The hall is long since demolished but you can still see the rather grand gateway that led to it. Walk along the river (the OS map shows the path going straight across the field) until you reach a stile into woodland that drops down to an ancient bridge on the river. The OS map shows the path crossing the river where there was once a wooden bridge but we'd recommend using the bridge that still exists! An ugly, unnecessarily-large sign advises you to then stay away from the river bank where you will trouble anglers, and stick to the path. There's just one problem – there's nothing to say where the path is! And there's no waymarker sign to help indicate direction. In fact you are heading for the large house at the end of a track to your right (looking away from the bridge). The footpath crosses a stile right next to the house. You may be nervous going so close to someone's front room but it's where the footpath goes. You'll see two waymarker signs on the fence in front of the house. Turn left to cross the stile and stick to the edge of the field for about 50 yards. Another stile will then take you into a small woodland. Keep to the trees (and to the left) for about 150 yards and eventually in the fence on your left

The bridge over the River Irt

IRTON : 81

Walk through the woods to the next stile

Follow track to the house (Vineyard) – the stile and path are right next to the house

you'll see a stile taking you into what is basically an overgrown ditch; in the old days it would have been called a 'syke'. Carefully wend your way up the hill – this is where a good crushing of reeds under foot will be helpful. About 75 yards uphill is another stile taking you back onto firmer ground. Where to go next? Look about 10 o'clock and you'll see on the top of the hill another stile – head for that. Cross that and the farm lonning and take the stile immediately opposite and – once in the field – turn right. Follow along the hedge, through a gate and then round the last field and into St Paul's Church, Irton. Enjoy the beauty of this church before heading back. You can reward yourself with a drink at the Lutwidge Arms in Holmrook.

The delightful Stock Bridge over the River Irt on the Gosforth to Irton corpse road

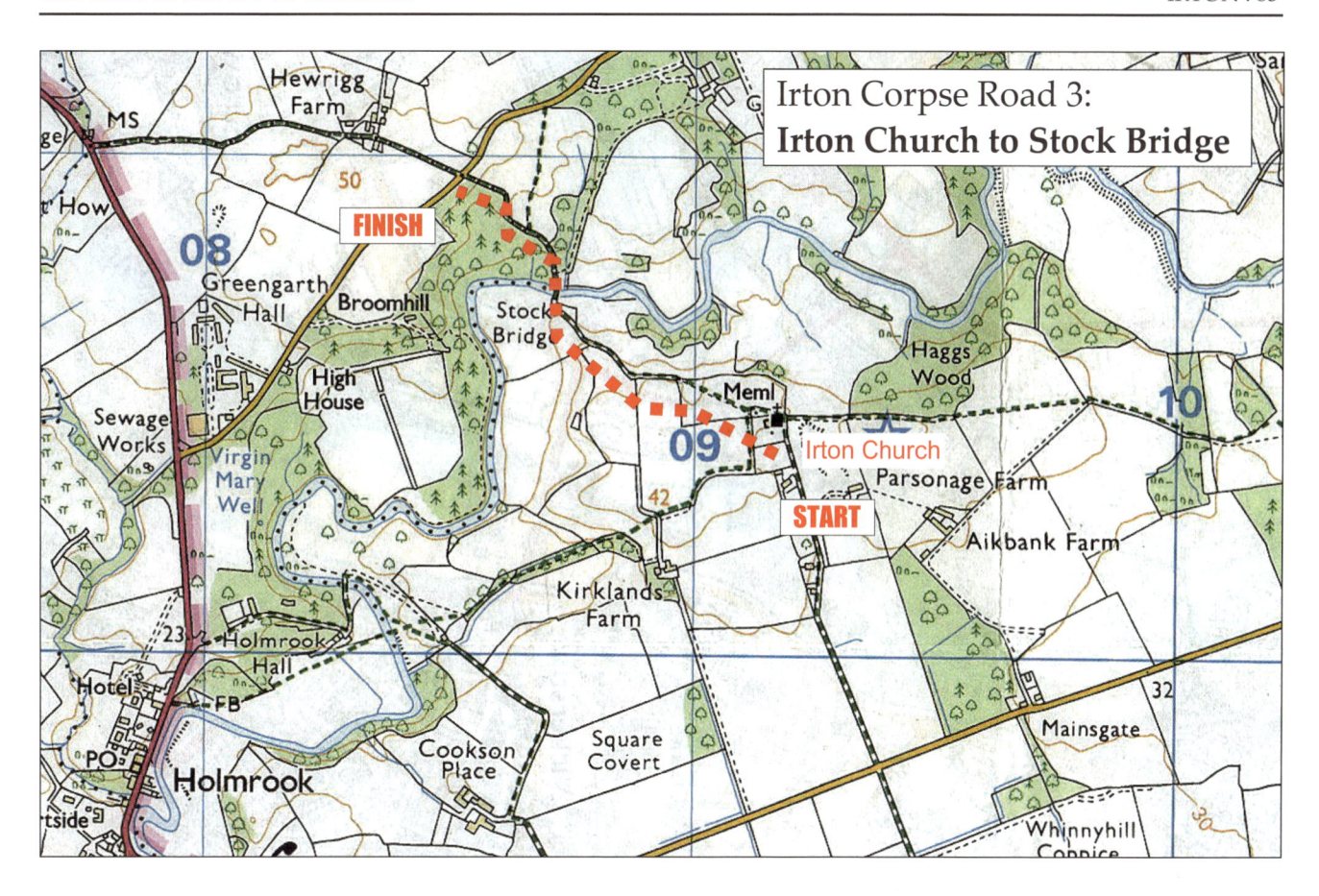

THE CORPSE ROADS OF CUMBRIA   IRTON : 83

Irton Corpse Road 3:
Irton Church to Stock Bridge

Irton to Stock Bridge

THIS is referred to in the 19th Century court records as the corpse road from Gosforth but as the first part is now the busy and dangerous A595 we don't suggest you start from there. Indeed we are advising walking this route in 'reverse' – ie from the church as far as the footpath just beyond Stock Bridge – and then retrace your steps back to the church. It is a short walk but takes you by the River Irt over the delightful Stock Bridge and through a shaded wooded lane.

DISTANCE: 1km

MAP: OL6 – Explorer

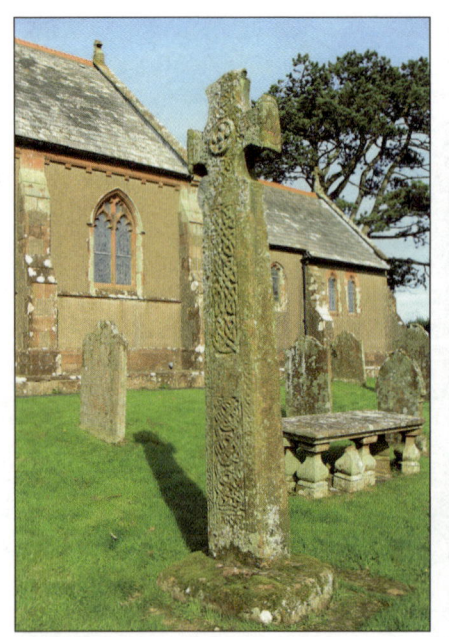

The Celtic Cross at St Paul's Church

GRADE: Easy but can get muddy.

THE WALK: As this is a walk best done in 'reverse', park or set off from

The path down to Stock Bridge

St Paul's Church, Irton. When you come out of the church turn left and the footpath is signposted from the right-hand gate. Go round the left edge of the field, heading for the opposite corner. The path drops down from this corner with a large hedge on one side and a drop down to the River Irt on the other side. This is reminiscent of truly ancient 'dykes' (hedges) or kests (raised banks) and one wonders if in the past this was the type of boundary that existed on both sides of the corpse roads around Irton. The path drops down to the impressive Stock Bridge. The size surely indicates the importance of this route in the past – or did people in the 18th Century just make bridges to last? It is worth crossing the bridge and wandering up through the beautiful wooded lane until you reach a single-track road. You can carry on to Gosforth via the path that goes through Newrigg Farm. For the brave you can walk up the A595 and carry on to Gosforth (remember to walk on the right hand side of the road, facing traffic if there is no path). If you do, the single track road on your left at the top of the hill goes to Hallsenna; this is Great Lonning and in Hallsenna itself is Little Lonning. You'll also pass at one point 'Squeezed Gut Lonning' but this is now so overgrown it is really just a hedge. Turn right at the brow of the hill to Meolbank (via the caravan park) and this is Gallows Hill which drops down to meet Low Lonning. However for this particular corpse road walk, we recommend turning back and retracing your steps to the church.

You have reached Stock Bridge – but it's worth walking a bit further

The sunken lane beyond Stock Bridge is well worth walking

Are you sitting comfortably?

WE have come across some mentions of the dying being laid or sat in a particular pose for their final moments. Rev Canon James Simpson in *Things Old and New at and around Kirkby Stephen* (1877) tells how a husband was encouraged to cease holding his dying wife in his arms and let her lay back and die, ending her suffering: *"Hush! Hush!' said an experienced matron to a husband who could no longer restrain a sob of agony, as he held in his arms a dying wife, and felt moment by moment that she was slipping away from him. "Hush! And disturb not the spirit in passing lest it struggle back, and has to stay twenty-four hours longer in mortal agony. Let her go when God calls her, it is best." And there was still silence, broken only by the laboured breathing of the dying woman, until the clock struck twelve. "There," said the matron in a low whisper, "the night has turned, she'll go now," and in a few moments the last breath was breathed, and the soul left its tenement of clay."*

More remarkably Brampton had its own high-backed chair in which people could 'die', the chair being lent out around the parish. Henry Penfold recalls this in a lecture in 1906: "Another strange belief which existed in Brampton until recently was in the efficacy of the death-chair... Persons nearing their latter end were supposed to die more easily in a sitting position and in this chair rather than in any other way. The chair was loaned out by sympathising neighbours, and it is not too much to say that hundreds of persons have died while sitting upon it. It is now some years since this gruesome relic was used, and in the interval the chair, along with other furniture in the same cottage, has been seized for debt."

Workington to Camerton

'Camerton – that most inconveniently of placed churches'

'As soon as a death is known to have taken place, the neighbours flock in and there is a continual visiting till the burial takes place. A few of the neighbouring females go to take tea. Their husbands visiting in the evening, where there are pipes and tobacco, bread and cheese, and ale'

— *Chancellor Walter Fletcher's Diocesan Book, 1814-1855 edited by Jane Platt*

THE Workington corpse road can boast a couple of suitably ancient-looking stone crosses still in place alongside its route. They are built into two houses at Cross Hill near its junction with Park End road and one has the date 1703 inscribed upon it. The oldest source we have found to evidence this as a corpse road is *The History and Topography of the Counties of Cumberland and Westmoreland*, edited by William Whellan, published in 1860. He writes: *"In a niche in an old building erected in 1703, at Cross Hill, Workington, is a small equilateral cross, said to have been taken out of a chapel erected there in the reign of King Richard I, by someone who went out with the king. Parties formerly, when bringing their dead to bury from the country, used to rest the bier

Just one of the delightful scenes en route to Camerton

&c at this spot, and a homily was read over the corpse before proceeding into the town." It's frustratingly lacking in detail (such as where the corpses were being taken to be buried) and of course he gives no reference to the vague statements about reading homilies or "someone who went out with the king".

Richard Byers in his definitive two-volume history of Workington published in 1998 repeats Whellan's account and adds "tradition also states that in olden times when a corpse was being brought to the town for interment, it was set down here for a short time".

And it is to rumour and local gossip we must turn for any more information on this corpse road. The

The 'corpse crosses' at Cross Hill, near the junction with Park End Road

ghost-story and folklore writers tell of an oral tradition that the corpse road led (at least until the 15th Century) through the grounds of Workington Hall and Mill Fields to Camerton and its "inconveniently situated" church of St Peter. In

Curious Tales of Workington, for instance, published by Derek Woodruff in 2009 he suggests a route as going "along the Corpse Road, now Park End Road, and through the Mill Fields to Camerton". No sources are given. Woodruff also talks about the chapel of ease being re-built in the reign of Richard II (1377-1399) – so some 200 years after Whellan says it was originally built in the reign of Richard I (or has Woodruff just made a mistake and he means Richard I?). He does add that Park End Road is supposedly haunted by a grey lady or ghostly nun which adds some colour to this horribly minimalist corpse road. And HC Ivison in *Supernatural Cumbria* is able to add a veritable cavalcade of ghosts along this corpse road and "ancient throughway" among them Roman soldiers, grey ladies, nuns, a headless horseman and Workington Hall's 'infamous White Lady'. Also of interest is a ghost that once haunted Camerton Hall (the previous ancient hall, not the current more modern structure).

W Jackson, giving a lecture at Workington Hall on June 16th, 1880 (and later printed in the Cumberland and Westmorland Archaeological Society journal) compared the appearance of the ghost as similar to the 'bright boy' ghost that haunts Cumbria's Corby Castle. He adds that there is even a local saying upon seeing a woman wearing bright clothing that she is "glorious and terrible, like Camerton Ha' Boggle".

Further reading

Supernatural Cumbria – HC Ivison
Curious Tales of Workington – Derek Woodruff

Workington – Richard Byers

The History and Topography of the Counties of Cumberland and Westmoreland, edited by William Whellan, published in 1860

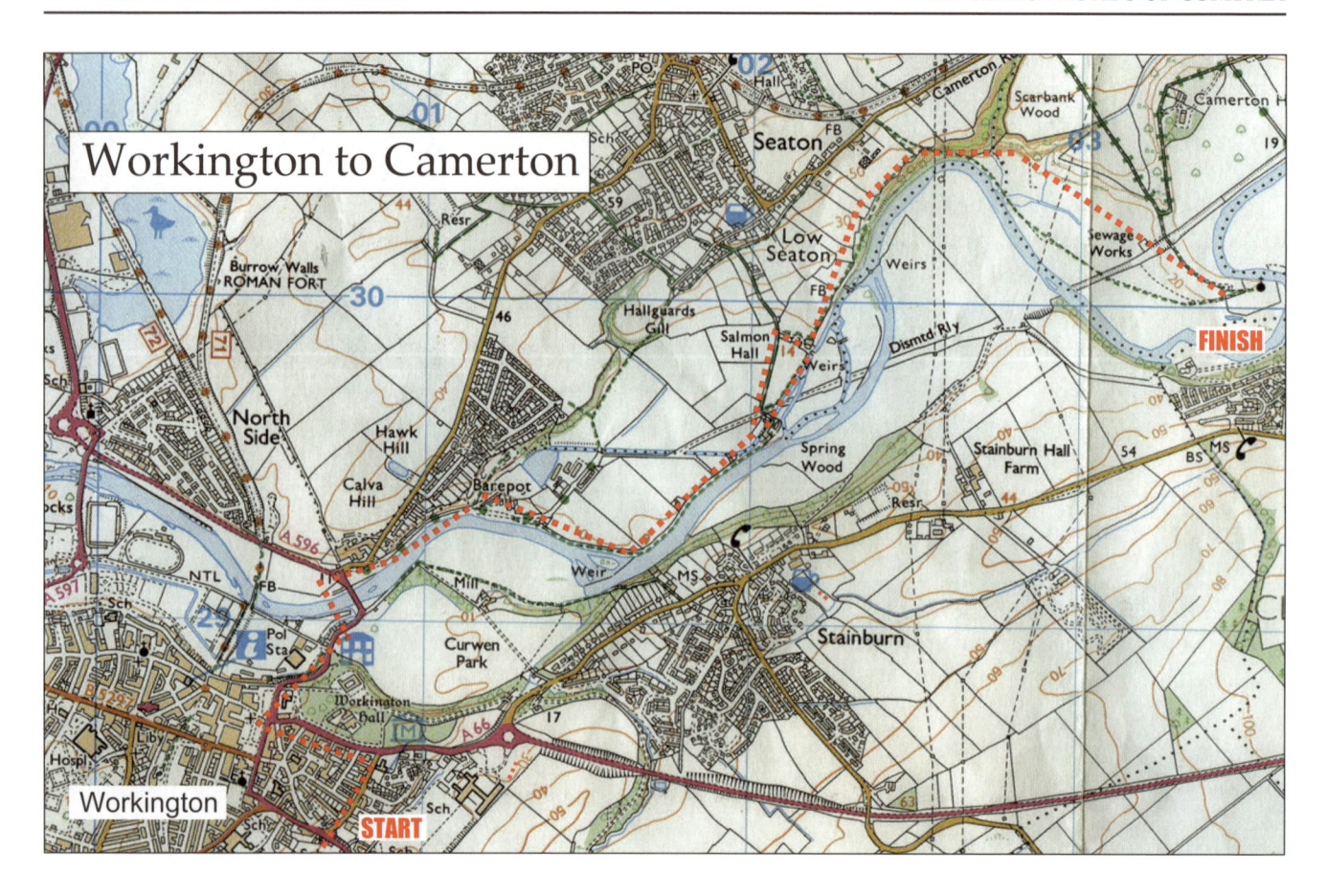

92 : WORKINGTON TO CAMERTON

THE CORPSE ROADS OF CUMBRIA

Workington to Camerton

Workington to Camerton

THIS walk takes you from the corpse crosses at Cross Hill, Workington, past the ruins of Workington Hall and following the River Derwent to Camerton. It's a walk that usually gives up a profusion of wildlife.

GRADE: Medium. There are a few stiles and a couple of steep climbs towards the end. The first part along the river bank is easy and, if you go via the road at first, the first half can be done by those in a wheelchair. The hard surface sadly runs out by the weir.

MAP: OL 303 – Explorer

DISTANCE: About 5.5km. Allow an hour there and an hour back

Not a coffin rest – just a wooden seat to help you catch your breath

THINGS TO SEE: The 'corpse crosses'; call in to the Helena Thompson museum which is on Park End Road; the ruins of Workington Hall; Mill Fields is a pleasant detour or a place to stop for a picnic – Friars Well, a less pleasant one; plenty of wildlife en route; Camerton Church is sadly usually locked but phone in advance if you want to see inside (see www.achurchnearyou.com/camerton-st-peter-church/).

THE WALK: There is a public car park next to Workington Hall but you can park anywhere in the town centre as it's only a short walk to the start. The crosses (pictured on p90) can be found at the junction of Cross Hill and Park End Road. Then walk north along Park End Road. On your right you will see Helena Thompson museum and opposite the end of the road is Workington Hall – or what is left of it. It's worth a quick look even though it is closed off to visitors. And it's certainly worth dropping down to Mill Fields below. Note: There are steep and irregular steps down through the woods but you can also drop down the main road (Hall Brow) to reach them. Opposite the police station and tucked into the side of Hall Brow is Friar's Well where legend tells a friar was murdered and his body dumped in the spring. But it is in a sorry state and not worth visiting except for historical interest. After your sojourn in Mill Fields you need to cross the bridge to reach the north bank of the River Derwent. There is a partial path along the south side but it runs out well before Camerton. Once on the north side, drop down again to the path along the river. It's easy to follow the path for a mile or so until

Friar's Well opposite the police station

The shameful condition of Friar's Well

Mill Fields, just below Workington Hall, are a slight detour from the corpse road but well worth a visit

Workington Hall: Home to several ghosts including Galloping Henry

Turn right at the measuring station and take the path through Seaton Mill. Or turn left and then first right down a well-made track (see map)

you reach the measuring station (pictured) where a lack of footpath signs (again!) means some care is needed. You can continue along the path through Seaton Mill by turning right after the measuring station. It can be daunting going through someone's backyard (!) and it is cobbled so you may prefer tu turn left then first right. After Seaton Mill you'll see two footpath signs – you want the one going straight on, following the wall of the house. You'll go through a couple of stiles and eventually meet up temporarily with the river again beside a pleasant bridge. (See picture on p89). This is a disused railway bridge and is closed to the public. Go through the stile on its left and past the house. On your right you'll now see a stile and footpath sign taking you across the field and into the woods. As one local described it to me, it's "very uppie and downie" but eventually you'll drop down through the woods and find yourself on the plain next to the river.

It's not clear where to go next but you are effectively heading diagonally across the field. Aim for the houses you can see on the side of the hill in the distance. The church is by the river so if you get confused, just follow the river. Don't be worried that you can't see the church; it is hidden behind trees. Halfway across the field is another redundant railway. It's worth looking behind you every now and again so you get your bearings for your return journey. At the other end of the field you will eventually see the church and the path leading to it.

The final stretch

St Peter's Church, Camerton

Although the church is usually locked, there are seats where you can recuperate and have your lunch before heading back the way you came.

St John's in the Vale

'The most picturesque placed church in the Lake District' – Canon Rawnsley

'A belief was at one time prevalent all over England that whatever route a corpse was carried became a public right of way'

– Northern Notes & Queries, Edmund Bogg, 1906

THIS is one of the most charming corpse roads in Cumbria as it takes you through the idyllic St John's in the Vale to its beautiful church. And once at the church you can sit by its holy well to eat your lunch before returning down the corpse road. It is according to Stephen Rycroft in *The Story of St John's-in-the-Vale*, a road that was used by people in the Vale to take their dead to Crosthwaite Church at Keswick. In 1767, however, the parishioners applied to the Bishop for a licence to give up the tough walk to Crosthwaite and instead start a burial ground at St John's chapelry (now church). Or as they put it, "several parts of the road from the said Chapelry to the parish church are often rendered dangerous and sometimes impassable by the sudden overflowing of the rivers from the mountains, and also in winter often filled with snow…". It's unclear which route they took to Crosthwaite but as we'll see, it seems those further south in the vale took a route via St John's church before it won its right to bury folk in a churchyard of its own. There is another chapel/church at Wythburn beside Thirlmere which dates back to the 16th Century. For the corpse road enthusiast or fit walker it would be possible to start from Wythburn but take the higher footpath, not the A591 which is a busy and dangerous road.

Local resident Keith Wren posted on Esmeralda's Cumbrian history and folklore blog in 2015 about the tradition he had heard about the corpse road stating: "I'd like to add another coffin path if I may. it's the

St John's holy well: The well can be found next to St John's in the Vale church

one which runs just above today's fell wall (probably formerly the head-dyke) along the eastern side of High Rigg in the Vale of St John (aka St John's in the Vale) This path was used to take the bodies from the Thirlmere valley to St John's in the Vale church during the period when Wythburn church had not yet received its licence to perform burials. It is quite possible that the corpse was carried in a loaned coffin fixed across the saddle of the horse, rather than in a cart (few, if any farms had carts because there were simply no roads *per se,* just trackways – sledges were used to carry loads). When the corpse arrived at the church it was taken out of the coffin and buried only in its shroud; this appears to have been a common practice in this part of Cumberland."

Mr Wren repeats the idea of a coffin somehow being strung across the saddle of a horse. By chance a colleague gave me a copy of *The Ballad of Blind Charlie*, probably written in the early 20th Century by Blind Charlie, real name Charles Robinson of The Naddle in St John's in the Vale. Charlie had been injured in a mining accident in Threlkeld in 1881 and a botched operation on his eyes left him blind. He had previously been sexton at St John's in the Vale and his biographical ballad includes these lines:

*"I was sexton at St John's i' the Vale
And had dug the resting-place
For a man whose name is not in my tale,
Who had run his mortal race.
I was bringin' the coffin on my horse
To lie in the church all night*

The corpse road through St John's in the Vale, near Keswick

The beautiful St John's in the Vale church

*A task, you may know, that takes two hands
To keep the load 'dead right'.*

He then goes on to describe how he's frightened by the fell gate apparently opening on its own. But it seems to confirm putting the coffin on a horse. One wonders how this worked in practice. If you needed both hands to keep the load "dead right" then how did you guide the horse?

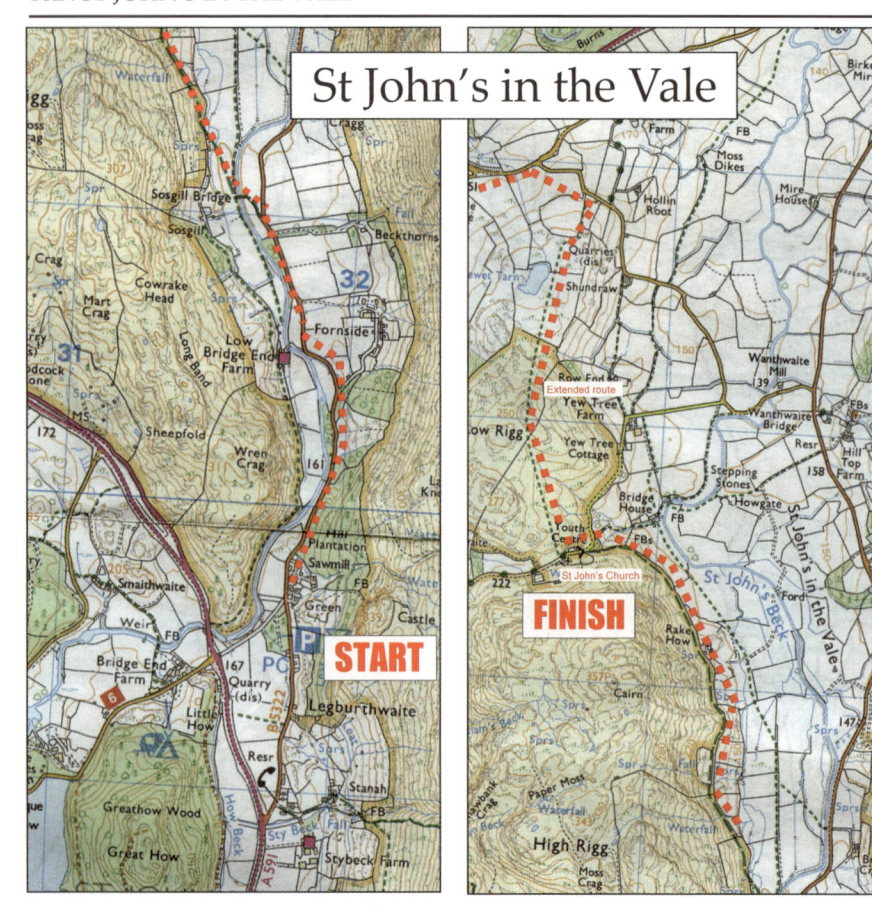

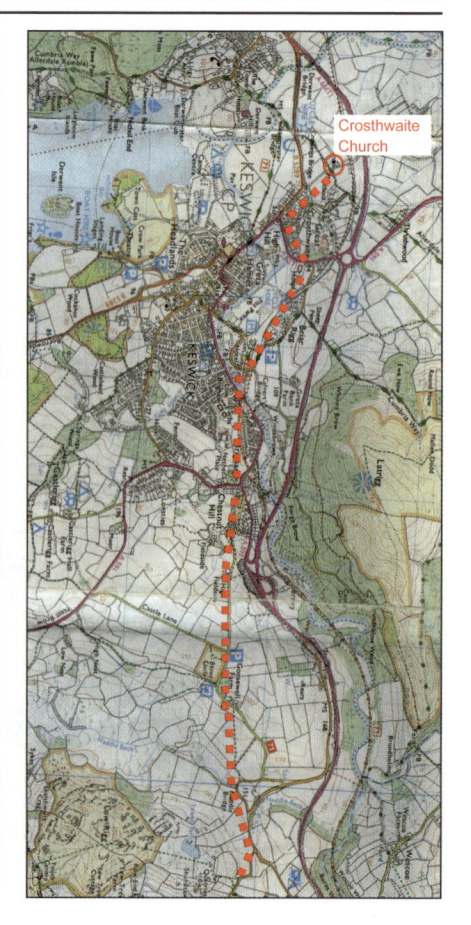

102 : ST JOHN'S IN THE VALE THE CORPSE ROADS OF CUMBRIA

St John's in the Vale

ANOTHER beautiful walk through the Lake District, under the pre-text of 'bagging' a corpse road.

GRADE: Easy

MAPS: OL4 & OL5 – Explorer

DISTANCE: 4km

THINGS TO SEE: The walk ends at St John's in the Vale Church. Beside the church you will see the recently-restored holy well.

THE WALK: Park at Legburthwaite car park (NY317 195) and follow the B5322 north for about half a mile. Remember to walk on the right hand side of the road so you are facing the oncoming traffic. Take a left turn over a packhorse bridge onto the footpath that is the start of the corpse road (I assume the original path would have followed the fellside further west). Climb up the footpath/corpse road till it joins the road to St John's in the Vale church at NY303 223.

For the enthusiasts, we have also shown on the map a scenic route that continues to Crosthwaite Church. It begins by heading out from St John's

St John's in the Vale – the view from the church

Church and crossing the fell; please note this involves some climbing over stiles in walls and the fell can be boggy – there is an alternative route by road. Once across the fell, you rejoin the road that takes you on to Eleventrees. You will pass Castlerigg stone circle – well worth a visit, not least because it is set in a natural amphitheatre making it one of the most picturesque stone circles in Britain. You turn right on the Penrith road to head into Keswick but we recommend taking the old railway through the town. We do realise this is probably not the route of the former corpse road – that is long lost – but it is much more pleasant than walking along the main road. This footpath skirts round the north-eastern edge of the town until you reach Crosthwaite Church; this church was also the final destination of the Borrowdale corpse road.

REFRESHMENTS: Served at The Lodge in the Vale about quarter of a mile south of the car park on the B5322. The farmhouse just north of the car park also sometimes serves refreshments. There is a cafe at the Keswick Climbing Wall at Eleventrees and plenty of cafes in Keswick itself of course.

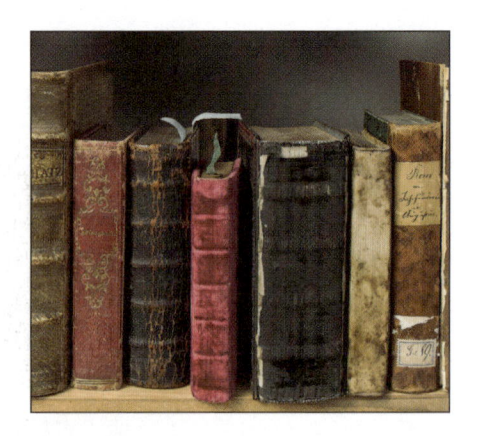

Further reading

Esmeralda's Cumbrian History & Folklore: esmeraldamac.wordpress.com
The Story of St John's-in-the-Vale by Stephen Rycroft
Rediscovering Our Past (A History of the Houses in the Parish of St John's-in-the-Vale, Castlerigg and Wythburn by Geoffrey Darrall.

The Night Watch

Laying out the dead in an age before undertakers

'It was formerly the custom when a person died and the body was laid out to have watchers through the nights which intervened between the death and burial'

– John Richardson, Keswick, 1876

THE undertaker is such an integral part of our society handling all matters related to death that it's hard to imagine what happened in the days before such a service existed. The role of laying out the dead was one usually left to women; the role of carrying the coffin to the funeral left to men. Indeed, it was often the midwife – she who had brought people into the world – who was also responsible for helping them leave it. Perhaps not surprisingly, there was much superstition and tradition surrounding these delicate moments. There still is but in the 18th and 19th Centuries we have records of complex and intricate rituals that were carried out by the community, some involving and sanctioned by the

Mrs Chambers still has the laying-out dress used for corpses by her mother. The dress is embellished with intricate lace work

Church (such as the ringing of the Death Knell) and others frowned upon as 'superstitious nonsense'. These rituals help people cope with the shock and bereavement following the death of a loved one. In many instances it gave the bereaved 'something to do' and also implied a set of rules which would ensure safe passage for the spirit of the deceased. We were fortunate to be contacted by Thérèse Chambers of Whitehaven about one aspect of these rituals. Her mother, Irish Catholic Rosina Kennedy, had been one of those responsible for 'laying out' the dead in Cleator Moor and she kept a box which included a laying-out dress, candles and crucifix. Fortunately, the dress has survived. Its beautifully intricate lace is indicative of the care and attention that must have been paid to the deceased. It is pictured on the previous page. Our grateful thanks to Mrs Chambers for allowing us to photograph the dress.

In 1876, John Richardson of Keswick gave a lecture about 'Old Customs and Usages of the Lake District' which gave more details about the hours before the 'lifting of a corpse' and its procession to the funeral. He said: "The funeral customs of the district although perhaps still capable of improvement have been greatly modified since the beginning of the present century. It was formerly the custom when a person died and the body was laid out to have watchers through the nights which intervened between the death and burial. These were always two of the nearest neighbours who sat in an adjoining

> **"The corpse is always 'laid out' upstairs and when the pall-bearers arrive it is customary to give them each a glass of whisky or rum before they bring the coffin, made by the local joiner, down from the bedroom"**
>
> – *The Sociology of an English Village: Gosforth* by W. M. Williams

room and went at stated intervals to snuff the candles which were kept burning near the corpse and to see that all was right."

These 'night watchers' are referred to in many accounts of Cumberland funerals in the 19th Century. For instance, the Rev Mr Kemble, vicar of Hesket, read a paper to the Carlisle Diocesan Conference in 1875 in which he said "it was the universal, and is now the occasional practice, while the corpse remains in the house decently prepared for burial, for relatives and friends to keep watch by it during the night, burning candles throughout the dark hours".

A glimpse into this most private of moments in a family's bereavement is given in a letter written by Dora Harcourt in 1820. She was staying with relatives near Whitehaven when a boy died and she 'with dread' went to call on the boy's family: *"All dread was, however, superfluous; nothing could be more peaceful or more exquisitely beautiful than the young boy's quiet features. A little mirror over the chimney-piece and several coloured prints, that hung around the room, I noticed were all covered by white cloths, and several young men and women sat round the body to secure its undisturbed repose until it should be laid in the grave."*

The mention of covering mirrors recalls the custom of ensuring, while

**"Stop all the clocks, cut off the telephone,
Prevent the dog from barking with a juicy bone,
Silence the pianos and with muffled drum
Bring out the coffin, let the mourners come."**
— WH Auden

the body is still in the house, that mirrors and reflective surfaces are covered. There appear to have been a couple of theories as to why this should be done. One school of thought says it was to stop the spirit seeing its reflection and becoming confused. Another that seeing your own reflection in a house of death was a portent of your own demise. Similarly clocks appears to have been stopped to ensure the departed soul did not become confused by earthly matters such as 'time'.

Henry Penfold writing in 1906 (CWASS) said: *"The laying out of the corpse is an important occasion, attended by sympathising neighbours. A curious custom at this time is that in the room where the body is lying all the glass is covered, particular care being taken that mirrors should be hidden with white cloth. This precaution is taken on the ground that it is unlucky for anyone to see the reflection of a corpse in the glass. Any clock in the room where a corpse lies ought not to be allowed to go during the time that the room is so occupied."*

Mr Penfold goes on to say about a most curious custom associated with laying-out the dead:

"In January of this year (1906) I had occasion to visit a cottage where a corpse lay. I was amazed to find on its breast a sod, the green side of which rested on the body. Upon the sod was a plate of salt. On enquiring the reason for this strange proceeding, I was informed that it was to prevent the swelling, or 'heaving', as it is locally called, of the dead body, and I was also mysteriously answered with the quotation 'Earth to earth'."

We have no evidence that this custom was widespread but it was not unknown.

Inside the chapel at Keld on the Mardale corpse road

Whitehaven resident John Skelly writing about his memories of the town in the 1920s suggests white sheets were used for more than just covering of mirrors:

"Here I might remind you of another custom linked with death. Whatever room the corpse lay in, that room was made to look all white. The walls being draped with white bed sheets pinned to the picture rail which ran around the room, or by some other means. These sheets were often borrowed from neighbours, some of even the poorer families kept them laid by in a drawer and however poor, were reluctant to use them for any other purpose. They were always in readiness for such an event since death was much more common then, especially among the young and with the many mining families."

Finally, we should note that it was considered necessary to kiss or touch the corpse laid out in the back room but whether this was out of respect or some long-forgotten superstition we cannot say.

Facebook

In June 2017 we posted on Facebook about customs when there is a death in the family and many said they closed blinds or drew curtains. Here is a selection of some of the comments received:

Josephine Pae: I still close my blinds. When I was little all the bearers and funeral director had a whisky before they set off.

Further reading

Funeral Customs: Their Origin and Development by Bertram S Puckle

Join the Cumbrian Folklore Group on Facebook for discussion on funeral traditions and other topics in the county

Joe Smith: The concept of closing the curtains was twofold – to ensure privacy of mourning relatives still inside the house (away from prying eyes) and as an outward indication – advance warning – to those visiting the home/passing on the street that a death had occurred inside.

Barbara Eslick: Close the curtains for immediate family members. When I was nursing we would open the window slightly, lay the body straight and leave for an hour before laying out to let the soul depart.

Pamela Woodall: Also close curtains on day of funeral of a neighbour.

Kelly-ann Gatenby: I always keep the blinds tilted for a week after. My

"Curtains were closed until after the funeral. My great grandmother was laid out in the 'front' parlour and pennies on her eyes and a saucer of salt on her belly. No idea about the salt but pennies stopped her eyes opening, I was 8 and it was 1954. We all had to view her! Remember it well."

– Pauline Hughes, Facebook November 2016

nan and granda always told us to do it to pay our respects. If I pass funeral cars on the road, I always turn my music off and slow down same when I drive into the crematorium.

Angela Parker Mean: When my uncle Freddie died a lot of the family visited him in his upstairs bedroom in an open casket with candles. We sat reminiscing, praying laughing and crying – sad but also a comforting experience. When my mum died close family members put things into the coffin for her to be buried with. I put a lock of my hair and a letter in as I'd taken a lock of her hair. It's now in my locket. We called for the local priest to support the family. We gathered at the home address, family and close friends tea or something stronger then made our way to church. Then our curtains were closed for a week.

Shelley Crowe: Where this is practical – no kids in the house, a space for the person – my family still do this.

Jeni Graham: Stop clocks and close blinds/curtains After funeral windows and blinds open. Clocks are started after 7 days

Lesley Thompson: Always open a window when looking after someone in their final hours and close curtains and draw blinds for family. Always say God bless when I see a hearse.

The grave of 18th Century 'magician' Dr Fairer at Orton Church. The inscription reads: "Under this stone lie the remains of Dr William Fairer, of Redgill, whom long experience rendered eminent in his profession and who was an instance that knowledge in the ways of death doth not exempt from its approach. Reader, in this thy day live well, that thou mayest have hope of a joyful resurrection, He died July 31st, 1756, aged 75 yeard."

The terrace path under Cat Bells with views across Derwentwater. Snowcapped Blencathra and Skiddaw are in the distance

Borrowdale to Keswick

A corpse road you can walk – or travel by boat

"Now, Lake-men, claim your right of way, and see the business done,
Come with your crowbar, spade, and pick;—and sure the battle's won"

— *Punch*, 1887

THE Kinder Scout mass protest of 1932 is rightly famous. In April 1932, nearly 500 people marched onto the moorland plateau overlooking Manchester. They were angry at the Duke of Devonshire's gamekeepers stopping people walking freely on Kinder Scout. Five of the protesters were arrested and jailed for up to six months. But the action and outcry over the arrests led to the rights to roam we enjoy today – and also to the eventual formation of Britain's national parks.

But lesser known is a similar mass protest that took place 45 years earlier in Keswick involving thousands of people. They were fighting landowners who had started locking gates and preventing access to the fells. Subsequent legal action prompted *The Manchester Guardian* to predict the "case will affect the right of ascent to almost every mountain in Britain". The protests centred on Latrigg and Fawe Park. It is the latter case that interests us as this was held up to be an old corpse road with all the legendary (and unfounded) rights that go with it. The corpse road led out of Borrowdale, skirting round the western edge of Derwentwater and ending at Crosthwaite church. The leaflet issued at St Andrew's Church, Rosthwaite (Borrowdale's church) tells the familiar tale:

"On November 8, 1765, the inhabitants of this chapelry were granted the privilege of having their own churchyard to relieve them of the 'great inconvenience, labour, expenses of carrying the dead along narrow tracks, especially difficult in flood or snow, the five miles and upward to Crosthwaite. The parson earning the sum of £26 a year, was required to take a true note of all burials, and the fees to Crosthwaite on a Saturday from time to time."

The walk through Borrowdale

The mention of the Borrowdale vicar collecting the fees and taking them to Crosthwaite echoes the compromise reached between many other villages and their mother church when petitioning for the rights to bury their own dead and do away with carrying coffins along corpse roads. The mother church was reluctant to give up the exclusive rights and lose the revenue from burials. Crosthwaite was also the mother church for people living in St John's in the Vale.

This ancient corpse road became the centre of national newspaper attention in 1886 when owner of Fawe Park, Mrs Spencer Bell, tried to close it. She ignored pleas from local people and ordered her gardener to fasten a gate across the track and erect barriers made of brambles and sticks. Rev Hardwicke Rawnsley of Crosthwaite Church took up the fight and revived Keswick's Footpath Preservation Society. On 30 August 1887, a gang of protesters headed for Fawe Park. They removed the barriers and marched en masse along the path. Mrs Bell at first erected bigger barriers to try to keep people out but eventually capitulated. The footpath remained open and in the 1970s the Ramblers Association – the 'descendants' of the Keswick Footpath Preservation Society – made the path part of the Cumbria Way: a 70-mile long-distance path that stretches the length of the county.

The fight for the corpse road through Fawe Park inspired a poem in the satirical magazine *Punch*. Here is an extract….

THE BATTLE OF THE WAY

"Now, Lake-men, claim your right of way, and see the business done,
Come with your crowbar, spade, and pick;—and sure the battle's won,
For bolts and bars show Spedding's race that you don't care a fig,
And prove that right's no match for might when rallied round Latrigg."

So shouted Routh-Fitzpatrick, and Lake-men with a cheer,
To Fawe Park Gates from Keswick's peaceful slopes were drawing near,
When high upon the topmost wall as if to break the spell,
There uprose the Solicitor of Mrs. Spencer Bell.

But Routh-Fitzpatrick heeded not his protest, nor replied;
So Mrs. Bell's Solicitor, he promptly stood aside,
And watched the next proceedings with a disapproving frown,
For up went crow-bar, pick, and axe, and gate and bar went down.

So onward towards Silver Hill advanced the active host,
And cleared each wire fence away, and levelled every post;
And when with crowbar, pick, and axe, they'd made their purpose plain,
To Nichol Ending they returned in triumph once again.

THE CORPSE ROADS OF CUMBRIA

BORROWDALE : 117

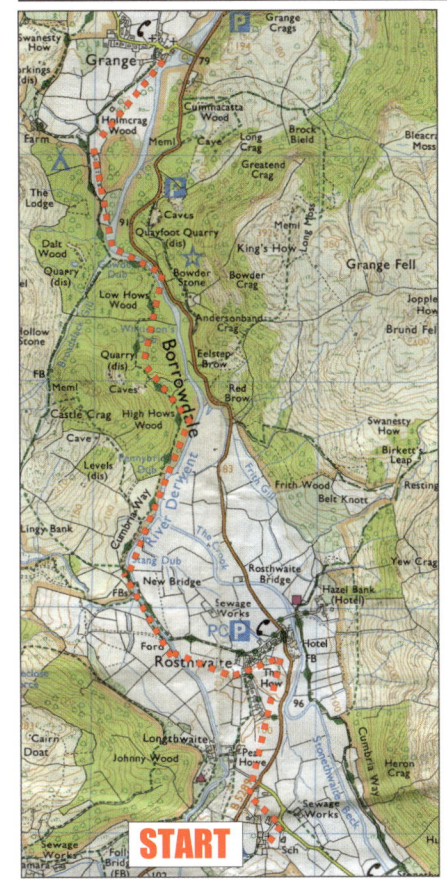

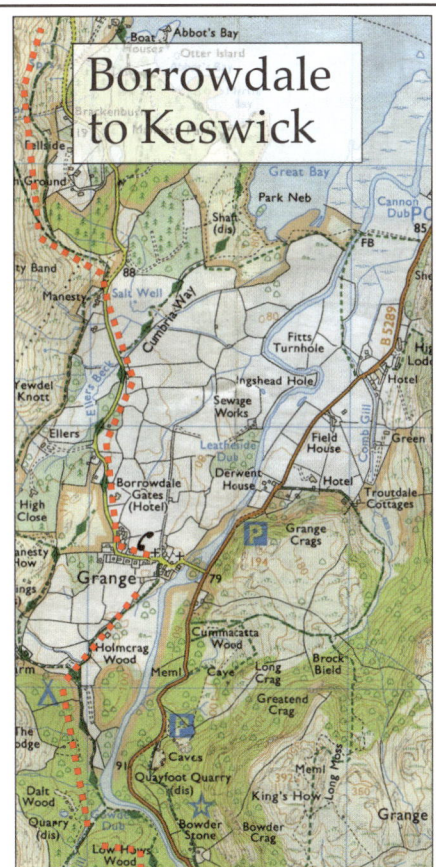

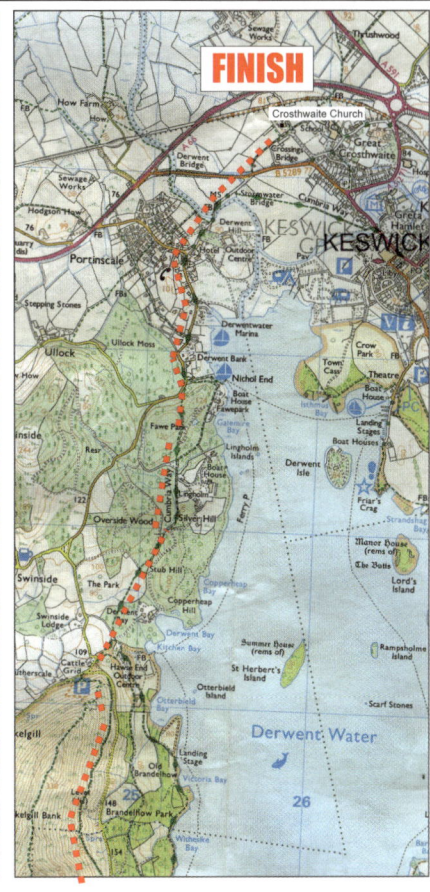

Borrowdale to Keswick

Borrowdale to Keswick

THE precise route of the corpse road is unknown but during the footpath protest in 1887, Canon Rawnsley claimed the path through Fawe Park was part of the old corpse road. This is logical as following the western side of the lake takes you directly to Crosthwaite.

GRADE: Moderate

MAP: OL4 – Explorer

DISTANCE: 12km. Allow a couple of hours and you may wish to return using the launch on Derwentwater or the bus. We have suggested a path along the terrace on the western side of the lake so you can enjoy the views over the lake and fells.

PARKING: There is a National Trust car park at Rosthwaite or you can use the village hall car park next door. You can also park in Keswick and catch the No. 78 bus to Rosthwaite.

REFRESHMENTS: There are plenty of cafes and pubs en route. We recommend the Flock Inn at Rosthwaite.

THINGS TO SEE: The slate workings in Borrowdale and the caves; or enjoy a trip on the Derwentwater launch. You will pass the Lingholm Estate near Fawe Park which has connections with Beatrix Potter including the kitchen garden which inspired Mr McGregor's Garden in *The Tale of Peter Rabbit*.

THE WALK: Start at St Andrew's Church in Rosthwaite (there's no village of 'Borrowdale'; the name refers to the valley). The church includes a small exhibition on the history of the valley but you'll also find a larger exhibition at the Methodist Church in Grange. Head back into Rosthwaite and head down the lane to the Flock Inn tea rooms (there are public toilets on your right). Continue through the farm and follow the lonning to the river (the Derwent). Follow the path east as it climbs into the woods. Eventually the path will lead you into Grange where you can stop for a break in one of the cafes. Head north out of Grange (see map) and pick up the terrace path at Manesty. It eventually drops into Portinscale and then head to Crosthwaite.

Knock, Knock

When death comes calling

"Hark, hark. Death knocks"

— Entry scribbled in the pages of Parish Registers of Barton, Westmorland in 1776

THE belief in audible death warnings is still strong with many — so wrote Cumbrian researcher Henry Penfold in 1907 and he went on to illustrate the prevalence of the superstition with a chilling tale: "A girl lay dying in a lonely country farmhouse. About midnight a loud resounding knock was heard at the front door. The girl herself heard it, and asked the relative who was watching by the bedside to go out and answer the summons. No one was found at the door. The same thing followed twice over at intervals of an hour or thereabouts. The patient remarked the wonderful character of the sounds, and said 'It is my death warning'. Shortly afterwards she died."

He gives a second example of a woman riding a white horse up to a cottage in Cumrew and rapping on the door before, presumably, vanishing. We too have heard of a tale involving death raps which occurred in the late 1950s or early

1960s at Hogarth Mission in Whitehaven. A man returned to the church when it was empty to retrieve car keys he had left there. He was about to pick up the keys when he heard a single note being played on the organ. Through a frosted pane in the church he saw the arm of a person and heard raps of someone knocking. The man left as fast as he could. The next day he heard at his workplace – Sellafield – that a colleague had died and believed that the ghostly visitation the night before had been a warning about this. Penfold adds that "Death warnings, according to those who believe in them, are not confined to one kind of sound. Rumblings, thumps, knocks, and other noises are all premonitory" and adds that "there is no more certain death warning, according to many, than the howling of a dog three times during the night". The Whitehaven boggle has not been seen in many years but the common story about the town centre ghost is that it is in the form of a black dog that howls outside your house at night as a warning of a death to come.

Rappings, of course, were at the heart of the Fox sisters case at Hydesville, near New York in 1848 when Kate and Margaret Fox claimed they were haunted by a spirit they called 'Mr Splitfoot' who kept making rapping noises in their home. They eventually came up with the idea of asking him to rap out their ages which he apparently did. This led to then

> **'A time honoured practice at funerals in the county was the wearing of white hat mournings by the men folk. During the funeral service they kept on their hats in church. On the first visit to the church after the funeral, which was usually the second Sunday thereafter, the men again wore their hats, complete with mournings, during the service'**
>
> – *Cumbrian Folklore and Customs* by Herbert and Mary Jackson

asking it to rap once for A, twice for B etc so it could communicate messages. This 'spirit rapping' sparked a craze for seances and rapping which is credited with encouraging the birth of Spiritualism.

Journey's End: Swindale Head where the corpse road routes for Shap and Mardale meet

Mardale to Shap

A popular walk from a 'lost' village

'At a funeral it was the custom to carry the corpse to the grave feet first, in the belief that this would prevent him from seeing his way back to the house in which he had previously lived'

– Lake District Folk Lore, Gerald Findler

YOU won't find the village of Mardale on the map. The village and its valley was flooded in 1935 to create the Haweswater Reservoir. That said, after a long, dry summer you will see the walls of Mardale rise ghost-like from the bottom of the receding reservoir. The corpse road, however, remains and is marked on Ordnance Survey maps and on signposts as 'Old Corpse Road'. As such, it only goes as far as Swindale Head even though it's always known as the Mardale to Shap corpse road. We'll take you the whole route to Shap but be aware that is a distance of nearly 11km – each way!

The true path from Swindale Head to Shap is also largely guessed since there are no records of its precise route. United Utilities whose predecessors flooded Mardale have kindly built single-track roads for much of the latter half of the route ensuring an easy path for those who need it.

The definitive work on Mardale is *Mardale – Echoes and Reflections of a lost Lakeland Community* by Shap Local History Society and it tells how Mardale was split between two parishes: Bampton for those living on the north and west of the valley, and Shap for those on the east and south. This needed the corpse road to Shap (and presumably one to Bampton) until the villagers petitioned in 1728 for their chapel of ease to be allowed to carry out burials too. Their petition contains the usual protest

The last stretch of the corpse road with St Michael's Church, Shap in the distance

about snow and floods at winter: *'The great distance from their parish churches which causes excessive expense for funerals and the souls as well as the bodies of infants taken to be baptised are endangered. To receive the sacraments, as befits sons of Holy Church, it is impossible without much toil and inconvenience, especially in the snows and floods of winter. They have no doubt about the consecration of the chapel, which has been used from time immemorial. They pay the curate reasonable fees and emoluments, as in the neighbouring chapelries. The chapel is well roofed and in proper repair. They undertake for themselves and their heirs to respect the rights and privileges of Shap and Bampton vicars, and to go on supporting a curate of their own. They humbly implore the bishop to grant a licence for burials, baptisms, marriages and any other rises of the church.'*

The request was granted and the registers record the last use of the corpse road to Shap: "June 7th 1736: John Holme of Brackenhowe, the last corpse carried from Mardale to be buried at Shap."

The route of the corpse road to Shap rises steeply out of the valley, offering dramatic views over the Haweswater reservoir. Once you have the steep climb out of your way, it's a gradual drop down into the Swindale valley and to Swindale Head. For many, that will be enough and you'll be happy to turn back. But for the real corpse road enthusiasts determined to follow it all the way to Shap, we have provided the route following a path suggested by 20th Century antiquarian Jim Taylor Page. It crosses to the south side of the valley to the farm of Tailbert and then on to the hamlet of Keld. At Keld you will find the chapel of ease still open to the public and cared for the National Trust. From Keld the path continues to St Michael's Church, Shap via the megalithic Goggleby Stone. This is a tough walk though so we also outline an easy path on the north side of the valley.

Mardale church before it was destroyed and the valley flooded to create Haweswater Reservoir

'The horse was young and skittish and broke away form the funeral party, turning back towards Mardale. A small child at the farm who had watched the departure of the cortege, saw the returning horse with its burden and shouted 'Mudder, Mudder, Ganny's cu' back'

– *Mardale Echoes and Reflections*

THE CORPSE ROADS OF CUMBRIA   MARDALE TO SHAP : 125

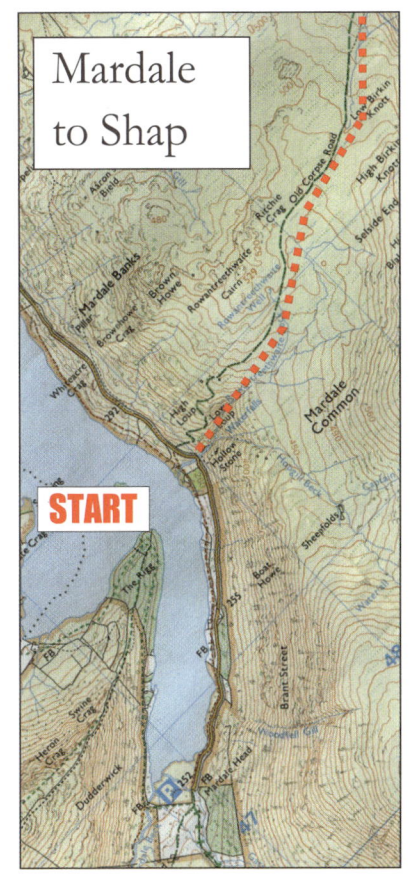

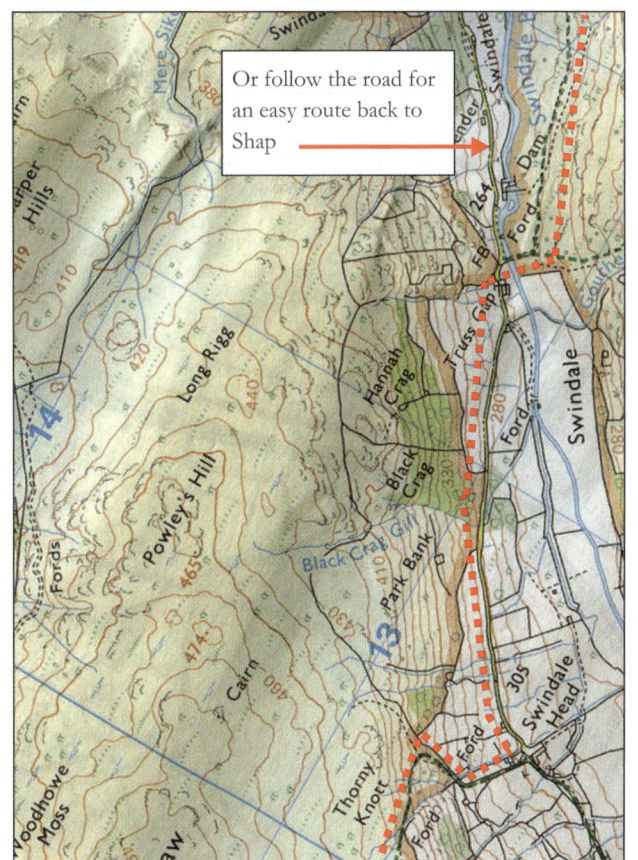

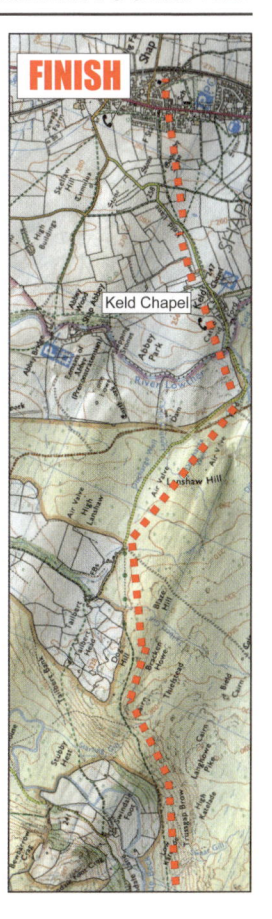

Mardale to Shap

START

Or follow the road for an easy route back to Shap

FINISH

Keld Chapel

Mardale to Shap

This is a long walk so we have split it into two: Mardale to Swindale Head and Shap to Swindale Head. The first starts with a tough climb and then a slog across the fell for which you will certainly need walking boots, a map, compass and know how to take a bearing. In contrast, the Shap to Swindale Head route is relatively easy though part of it still crosses the fellside so again a map and compass should be taken.

Grade: Difficult

Map: OS5 – Explorer

Distance: 10.5km. The signpost tells you the path from Mardale to Swindale Head is two miles. Don't

Inside Keld chapel

believe it! It may be two miles as the crow flies but there's a climb of about 500ft en route. Allow about three hours there and back (further hour and half if you go on to Shap). Shap to Swindale Head is about five miles but there's not much climbing involved. We'd suggest still leaving about three hours in total for a walk there and back.

Grade: Shap to Swindale Head is easy enough for walkers and families. The Mardale to Swindale Head requires map, compass and knowing how to take a bearing.

Parking: There is a public car park if you start from the Haweswater Reservoir (Mardale) end. There's no parking at Swindale Head but there is public parking at Shap.

Things to see: En route you can call at Keld Chapel (National Trust). You'll also be able to see the Goggleby Stone just outside Shap. And at Shap there is St Michael's Church and, in the village, there is a local history display at the Heritage Centre based in the Market Cross. There are cafes and pubs at Shap. If you're going to Mardale, there's the Haweswater Hotel but also a damn fine tea shop – and a good pub – in Bampton. This village was made famous in the film, *Withnail and I*.

Shap to Swindale Head: We have suggested parking at Shap and walking to Swindale Head as parking is easy in the village. It's well worth taking time to visit St Michael's Church and the heritage centre (Market House) in Shap. There's also cafes, pubs and a famous chip shop in Shap to find refreshment. Start your walk at the church and follow the path (see map on p125) across the fields. The path takes you past the Goggleby Stone which is believed to have once been part of a prehistoric avenue of standing stones, perhaps leading to the site now occupied by St Michael's Church, Shap. You'll eventually end on a single track road that will take you into Keld. This charming hamlet has a 17th Century chapel of ease which is open to the public and is well worth a visit. And 'ease' is precisely what you will need on your way back after your long walk! There has been claim and counterclaim about whether this was a chapel (it was) and whether it was related to the corpse road (almost certainly). Continue to follow the single track road and you will be taken out onto the fell. At Tailbert you will then need to get your map and compass out as you leave the well-made track and attempt to follow the path up the side of the fell (you will note there is an alternative route to Swindale Head which takes you along well-made single track roads. This is ideal if you are unsure of walking the open fell – but it is rather dull). You will follow the path about halfway up the fell before it eventually drops down towards a wooded area, skirts round that and then you head to the modern ford over Swindale Beck. Cross the beck and turn left, following the road to Swindale Head. Stop for your 'bait' (picnic lunch) and then make your return to Shap.

The Goggleby Stone near Shap – thought to be the last remaining stone from a megalithic avenue

Mardale to Swindale Head Walk:
This is the other half of the Mardale to Shap corpse road and we recommend starting at the 'Mardale' end (Haweswater reservoir) as parking will be easier. A final reminder that this is a tough climb and you need to know how to take a bearing as the path all but disappears on top of the fell. But don't let that put you off! If you are going walking you should be able to use a map and compass – it's safer and means you can explore the landscape better. Take a few minutes on YouTube or ask an experienced walker to teach you to take a bearing. The Ordnance Survey website has instructions but best to practise on landscape you know before you head into the unknown.

And the rest: It may be two miles on the map as the crow flies but this is the start of a long uphill struggle that will take an hour and a half to walk

For the Mardale walk, drive down the county's longest dead end: The road from Bampton to Mardale Head! You'll drive along the side of Haweswater Reservoir, past the Haweswater Hotel. There is a public car park at Mardale Head and then it is a short walk back to the start of the corpse road. However, there are a couple of lay-bys closer to the corpse road path if you wish to save your energy for the tough climb ahead. The path is sign-posted from the main road. This is the last sign-post you'll see before Swindale Head. The climb to the top of the fell is very tough but the views from the top make it worthwhile. Near the top are two derelict stone cottages – an ideal spot for a picnic before continuing over the fell. It's from this point you'll need to take a bearing as the path will soon disappear to almost nothing. It's worth noting any pathside boulders, cairns or posts en route to act as markers on your return. We always stop to look behind us so we know what the view should look like on our return. Once over the top of the fell, you will start to descend and the dramatic views of Swindale valley appear in front of you. Watch out for the small wooded area beside Swindale Head Farm and head for that. You don't go into it but instead head to the left of it (north) and follow the drystone wall down to a gate and a lonning leading to the farm. There you can rest and have a break before heading back – or if you are superfit, carry on to Shap.

Looking down from the corpse road on to the lonning leading to Swindale Head farm.

Further reading

Mardale: Echoes and Reflections of a lost Lakeland Community – Shap Local History Society
Spirit Roads – Paul Devereux 2013. Includes details of the corpse road route suggested by Jim Taylor Page

Websites

Shap History Society: https://shaplocalhistorysociety.wordpress.com/

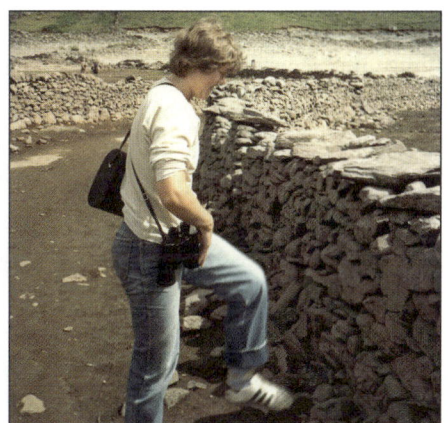

The lost village of Mardale rises from its sunken grave during a drought in 1984

Corpse candles and death lights

An exploration of luminous phenomena

'A corpse candle or light is a flame or ball of light, often blue, that is seen to travel just above the ground on the route from the cemetery to the dying person's house and back again'

– Wikipedia

WHEN a farmer vanished in West Cumbria in 1869 many villagers gathered on the fellsides to watch for his 'death light' so they could find his body (*Whitehaven News* June 5th 1930). It was believed "they would be able to locate the body by seeing the 'corpse candle' burning over it". These death lights, (also called corpse candles although this came to refer more specifically to the candles put beside a corpse after death and before burial) are a part of many cultures around the world although the meaning of them varies.

In north Cumberland at the end of the 19th century it was a "general belief that on the death of any person, his spirit, with the form and colour of a faint flame, passed along the 'burial road' to the church, and up to where the coffin would rest. Thence it was believed to go to the grave, where, in the case of a good man, it sometimes allowed itself to be seen again" (*Lancashire Evening Post* – Friday 10 March 1899).

Henry Penfold writing in 1907 (*Cumberland and Westmorland Antiquarian and Archaeological Society* 2nd series, vol 7) added more detail saying: "The belief in death-lights, or 'deed leets', once a common article of faith with many, is now confined to a very few, and these old persons. A death-light has been described to me as a 'blue lowe' about three feet high, which leaves the house the moment death has taken place and traverses the road that the funeral will follow. It enters the church under the door, and stands on the exact spot where the coffin will stand, flooding the building with light. Out of the church

Dobbie Bank, leading off Dobbie Lane in Cark. The road got its name from a dobbie (ghost) seen wandering along it in the 19th Century

The children in my day were not above making turnip-lanterns to keep off the boggles on All Souls' Eve, but I don't suppose they do it now. They thought less about the boggles than about scaring one another; and today all kinds of child's play, including practical joking, is made so easy. Making a turnip-lantern is not easy. Take a large turnip and remove a slice from the top. Carve out two eyes and a row of teeth, and place a lighted candle inside. Then fix the lantern on a pole and drape the erection in a sheet. The fixing of the pole must not disturb the seat of the candle within, and the sheet must not cover the candle's draught-hole at the top.
— *English Lakeland* by Doreen Wallace, 1940

Candlesnuff fungus – Xylaria hypoxylon – We came across it in Huntingstile Lonning, Grasmere. It is bioluminescent

it eventually comes, and makes its way to the spot where the grave will be dug, and ends its career by sinking into the ground there." He notes however that seeing a death light was a good omen as it showed the soul was departing in peace. He also adds this anecdote which we feel we should reprint:

"*A weird account of a death-light was given me by a friend whose father had the fortune, or misfortune, to see it. He met it as he was returning home one evening, and boldly endeavoured to stop its progress to see what the light really was. He succeeded for a few minutes in preventing its advance, but in an unwary moment he let it pass; it slipped between his legs, and sped its onward course to the churchyard. The sequel to so much foolish bravado, as may be expected, was most serious. Two days afterwards, when the funeral came to the spot where the encounter had taken place, the horse drawing the hearse stopped, absolutely refusing to move an inch. The difficulty was only got over by taking the coffin from the hearse, and passing it between the legs of the man who had barred the way to the death-light. After this had been done no further trouble occurred, and the procession arrived safely at the church.*"

In British culture at least a strange light seen at night is inevitably associated with the spirit of a dead person or the light from some wandering ghost. So Jennifer Westwood and Jacqueline Simpson report in *Lore of the Land* (2005) that "Orton, in the early 19th century was haunted by a boggle who appeared as a glowing amorphous shape. Like other boggles, it would lie in wait for

Dismissing mysterious lights as will-o'-the-wisps may simply be explaining one mystery away with another

late travellers".

In Cark in the early 19th Century a strange light was on occasion seen in a lane that went through the grounds of Cark Villa. This lane is now known as Dobbie Lane (see picture on p133). Author James Stockdale told in *Annals of Cartmel* how his brother had encountered the dobbie: "The light (and a most unnatural-looking light it was) came flickering down from the top of the wall into the middle of the road, and on his approach ran before him at about ten yards' distance, along the middle of the road, till my brother, in some astonishment, stood still; when it at once passed along the ground across the highway and up the wall, placing itself on the top a second time".

Beware of falling into the trap of dismissing such reports as the delusions of 'country bumpkins' from an uneducated age who merely mistook a 'will-o'-the-wisp' for a ghost. To call such phenomena as 'will-o'-the-wisp' is simply to call one mystery by another name. Scientists are generally unconvinced by the idea of self-igniting 'marsh gas' explaining such sightings – for what causes flammable gas to self-ignite?. And the suggestion it could last for more than a second or two indicates the need for a lot of gas or a 'wick'.

Further reading

Earthlights by Paul Devereux, 1982
The Penguin Guide to the Superstitions of Britain and Ireland By Steve Roud, 2006
Annales Caermoelenses Or Annals Of Cartmel by James Stockdale, 1872
The Lore of the Land by Jacqueline Simpson and Jennifer Westwood, 2005

Flookburgh to Cartmel

The priory was not built for the needs of man but for the glory of god

"It is quite astonishing how tenaciously people in former days held to what was called 'the corpse road'."

– Annals of Cartmel

WE can offer up a silent prayer to local historians like James Stockdale (1803-1874) for their good work in recording details about life (and death) in their parishes. James lived most of his life on the Cartmel peninsula and wrote *Annales Caermoelenses, Or Annals of Cartmel* in 1872. It includes much on the customs surrounding death and funerals, mentioning the strong belief in corpse roads and detailing one that ran from Flookburgh to Cartmel.

He writes: "It is quite astonishing how tenaciously people in former days held to what was called 'the corpse road' and how 'unlucky' it was thought to be to depart from it. The Corpse Road from Flookburgh to Cartmel Church is not by the direct road through Cark; but by the 'Green Lane' and on one occasion I remember a great squabble taking place when a corpse (that of one of the family of Mr Jopson of Myerside) was carried through the folds of the two farms at Green – though this really was the Corpse Road, and not the present road round the two barns there, this last road not having been in existence till some time after 1796, when it was made by the Cartmel Commons' Enclosure Commissioners."

James Stockdale furnished some detail on how the dead were carried on the corpse road. He states the corpse was always carried on the shoulders (perhaps in a coffin) although in the neighbouring parish of Furness they used sledges (biers) but notes "in passing over the fords of rivers, the corpse has been known to have been washed off the sledge, and lost for a considerable time". In Alexander Craig Gibson's book, *From The Old Man or Ravings and Ramblings Around Coniston* (1849) he states: "Rising a short ascent called, no one knows why, Doe How, you soon reach another cluster of dwellings, named Bowmanstead, the most prominent amongst which are the Baptists' Chapel and the Ship Inn; and beyond them, a row of houses which had its name from a somewhat odd incident. There was formerly an open ditch, called locally a syke, across the road here; and once the funeral array of a man named Jenkin, on the way to Ulverston, then the only place of interment for this part of the parish, had got near to Torver, when the mourners discovered that the coffin had slipped, unobserved, from the 'sled' it was carried upon, and, deeming it unseemly to proceed without it, they returned, and found it here in the syke, hence the spot is called 'Jenkin Syke' to this day."

Flookburgh to Cartmel

This is an easy 3.5km walk (Map OL7) and one that is accessible to everyone as it is on single track road all the way. We are grateful to Nick Thorne, countryside access adviser of the Lake District National Park Authority, for correcting an error in our first edition of this book. As Stockdale says, the route went from Flookburgh via Green lane to Cartmel (not via Cark). Mr Thorne adds: "Green Lane itself is the road that runs southwards from the Green to Flookburgh, whereas north of The Green it is called Birkby Road (or it was in the 'olden days' anyway). The first hundred yards or so northwards was created out of open common during the 1796 enclosure process and was called 'Green Road'. (And just to confuse things further, today Green Lane actually continues eastwards from The Green to Boarbank, although this, I think, is a relatively modern change). The Enclosure Award had this as Templand Road – and Stockdale was keen on the Enclosure process, so would have been familiar with, and used, those names. So, I reckon the corpse route would have been from Flookburgh Market Cross, eastwards for 50 yards or so, then left into Green Lane, past The Green and on up Birkby Road to Cartmel."

Which of course makes perfect sense and is indicated on our map opposite. The start is the market cross at Flookburgh. Headless Cross is just outside Cartmel and is suggestive of a coffin rest or wayside cross. It is pictured on page 140.

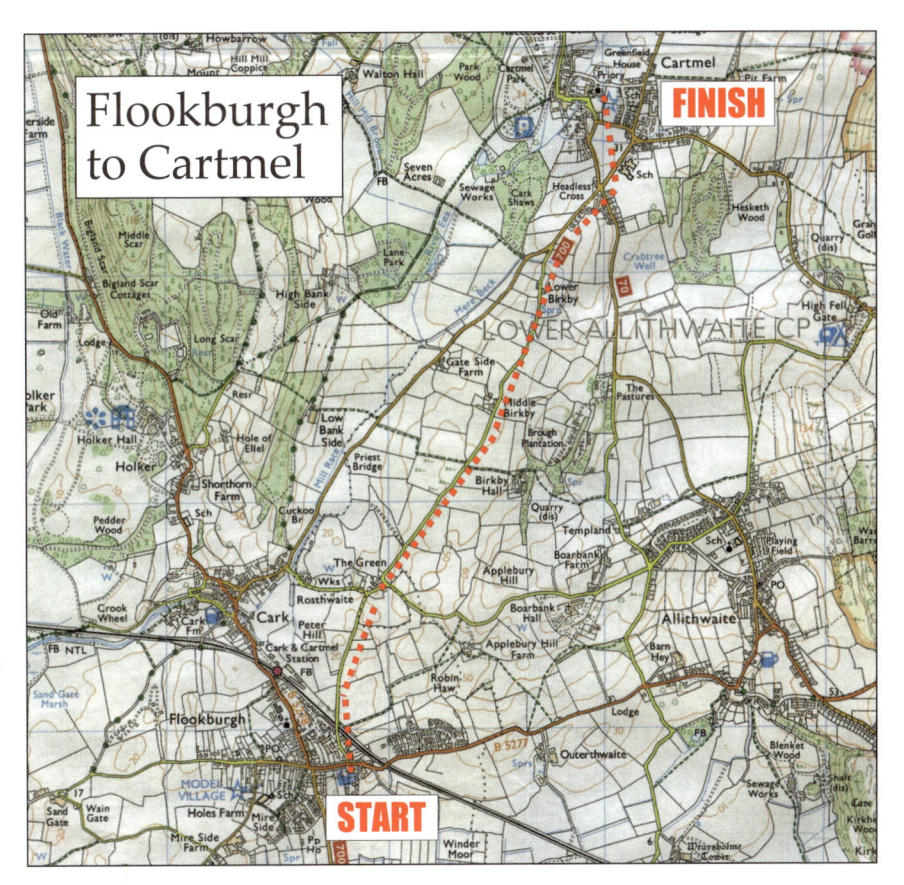

140 : FLOOKBURGH TO CARTMEL

THE CORPSE ROADS OF CUMBRIA

The Flookburgh to Cartmel corpse road with Cartmel Priory in the distance. Inset Headless Cross (*Peter Douglas*)

Can we all please just cheer up

A look at the changing fashions in funerals

'Death doesn't frighten me. It's what comes after.'

– Terry Pratchett

IT was quite clear and straightforward in my childhood (the 1960s and 1970s): Death was bad news. A sombre occasion in which you walked round for days in a hushed silence and at funerals you wore black. It's epitome was probably the funeral of Diana, Princess of Wales in 1997 – a truly sombre state occasion. But even at this there were perhaps hints of change. As the funeral began some women were heard to wail and cry out loud. This was never done at Christian funerals but Diana's popularity spread across cultures – including those where a public out pouring of grief was not only acceptable but expected.. The other 'fashion' that came into prominence at Diana's funeral was throwing roses onto the hearse as it processed through the streets. The driver had to stop a few times to clear the flowers so he could see the road ahead. But at some time after this iconic event, the growing trend for funerals being more 'celebrations' of someone's life became more prominent. There were requests from some families that black should not be worn at the funeral. Minute silences – usually so perfectly observed at football matches – became 'a minute of applause' and seemed to become the norm following George Best's death being marked in this manner. In the last few years, younger people have been releasing Chinese lanterns or balloons into the air though both of these have quickly gone out of fashion again; the first because the lanterns could land anywhere and set light to things; the second because of the harm to animals and the environment caused by bits of rubber left to rot. *The Guardian* reported (May 8th 2017) on the changing trend away from solemnity and towards a celebration. It told how funerals can be themed to the family's wishes and have included Spiderman, Darth Vader and She-Ra: Princess of Power costumes. There's a curious parallel arisen in recent years to the funeral road too: some journeys to the church or crematorium will pass – and even stop for a moment – at the pub, sports club or favourite spot of the deceased. It echoes the funeral rests of ancient corpse roads.

Some of these modern funeral traditions may seem shocking but it's worth remembering that funeral traditions change all the time – and probably faster than we think. It's a mistake to say "In olden times people used to do this…". They may have done it for a a few years or even a few decades but then the fashion will have changed. The Rev Mr Kemble reported to the Carlisle Diocesan Conference in 1875 on the funeral customs then prevalent in

Just one of the more unusual and fun coffins now being offered. This one from www.crazycoffins.co.uk

Cumberland, including the ones dying out and his plea for new practices to be adopted; in particular that funerals should cease being so morbid! As to those practices dying out, he tells of family and friends keeping watch over the body the night before burial with the burning of candles including "along the Fellsides". This notion of having candles lit on the fellsides is rather surprising and we can find no other reference to this so we wonder if Mr Kemble misinterpreted something he heard. However, it is interesting that it echoes the modern use of candles including in Chinese lanterns among today's youth. He also tells of funeral cakes "costing threepence or fourpence each, consisting of two layers of paste with currants between which used very generally to be given

Releasing Chinese lanterns became popular at the turn of the 21st Century particularly with young people but fell out of favour when the fire risk and harm to animals and environment were highlighted. They also resulted in spurious UFO sightings. Picture: Adam Wilson

at the house before the burial" but says this appears to have "entirely died out".

The Victorians anguished over the correct etiquette of wearing or not wearing hats at funerals and Mr Kemble comes down firmly against retaining hats during the funeral procession and in the church. In Victorian times a black mourning band would usually be worn around a top hat at funerals. Mr Kemble also dismisses the custom of a proclamation in the graveyard that there were to be refreshments in the nearby public house as "objectionable". Overall he is against many morbid practices and calls for a more 'cheerful' aspect.

Bassenthwaite to Caldbeck

A corpse road following the path of the Cumbria Way

"History is women following behind with the bucket"

– Alan Bennett, The History Boys

HISTORY is disappearing through the cracks in the floorboards at an alarming rate. And this corpse road has been caught just in time. As far as we're aware, this will be the first written account of this corpse road which we stumbled across in one of those typically serendipitous moments. We had just put the first edition of this book to bed and attended a music event at Bassenthwaite parish room. During the interval we were looking at a millennium map the village had published – and in one corner it showed the 'corpse road'! We were unable to add this to the first edition so are happy to include it now. The corpse road starts in the south-east corner of the parish near to (and running through) Barkbeth farm. Farmer Malcolm Ewart added a vital piece of the jigsaw when he told us that his grandfather had always said an old dilapidated barn on the path was once an Inn that had been used by the pall-bearers as a place to eat, drink and stay the night. The corpse road is said to continue to Caldbeck – a distance of nine miles. Without any other evidence this was just an oral tradition. So it was with some delight that several months later we came across Tony Vaux's newly-published comprehensive history of Caldbeck. In *Caldbeck: A Special Part of Lakeland* (2018) he says: "…many centuries later people in Caldbeck continued to tell a story about a ghostly woman who appeared dressed in white at the foot of Flatt Lonning, a lane used to carry corpses to the Caldbeck churchyard from the hamlet of Fellside". Fellside is to the south of the village and it's quite possible this is a memory of the road coming up from Bassenthwaite to St Kentigern's church in Caldbeck. It's particularly nice that it also has a ghost! Although the precise route is lost we've followed the Cumbria Way, a long-distance path created in the 1970s by members of the Ramblers Association (Malcolm Ewart says the corpse road originally headed south-east from the farm onto the fell). And Vaux also mentions another possible corpse road entering Caldbeck from the north through Brownrigg Farm. Flatt Lonning ran south from the B5299 near to Stadle Dykes.

We hope further research fleshes this corpse road out but there's no doubting that it's one of the more enjoyable – if exhausting – walks.

This dilapidated barn at Barkbeth was, according to the farmer's grandfather, once an Inn where pall-bearers rested en route to Caldbeck

Figure 1

Figure 2

Figure 3

The confusing part of this corpse road is when it goes through Barkbeth farm. As you reach the farm you'll see the gate (fig 1) which says Bridlepath on it. Go through that and head for the farm (fig 2). The old barn on the right is the former Inn used by corpse road travellers in times gone by. Turn left at the end, then right. Then go through the gate by the side of the modern barn (fig 3) and turn right at the end.

Distance: About 15 kilometres
Grade: Difficult, mainly due to its length but there is also some hard terrain. However there is a B-road that runs from Bassenthwaite to Caldbeck which is an easier alternative.
Maps: OL4 and OL5

Start: There is a small parking bay at the start but this is also used by climbers heading up the back of Skiddaw. The B-road that runs alongside the path to Caldbeck has a number of parking spaces.
Remember: Don't block gates.
The route: We have not included the complete route as it's 15km long but it follows for the most part the Cumbria Way. We have picked out the beginning and the end – though you can walk this either way of course.
Refreshments: Caldbeck is resplendent with cafes and a pub. There is also good parking but it gets busy in summer.

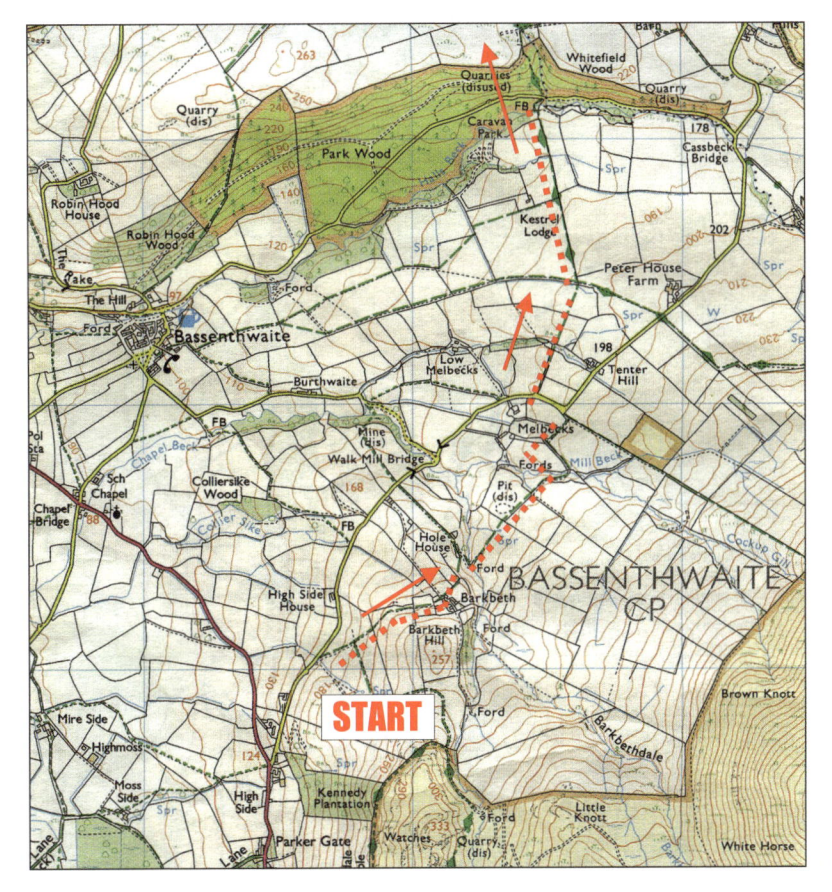

THE CORPSE ROADS OF CUMBRIA BASSENTHWAITE TO CALDBECK : 147

START: There is a small lay-by near the start. Do not block gates. You start by heading up hill; keep dogs on leads as there are sheep in these fields. Over the crest you will reach Barkbeth Farm. The public footpath goes through this (see previous page) and drops down into the valley to join the Cumbria Way (shown on the map as the green line with diamond-shapes on it). Follow the Cumbria Way to Caldbeck.

Park at 90 degrees if you can in lay-bys so more cars can use the available space

148 : BASSENTHWAITE TO CALDBECK

FINISH: When you arrive at Fell Side, you can continue on the Cumbria Way to Caldbeck but the oral tradition is that the corpse road came into Caldbeck via the route indicated. Flatt Lonning no longer exists so we have used the parallel lonning, Dickie Lonning; this was named after Richard Harrison who married Mary Robinson, the 'Maid of Buttermere', (died 1837) a famous beauty tricked into marrying the already-married John Hatfield.

Watch for the spitting stone: Spit in it and don't look back and your wish will be granted!

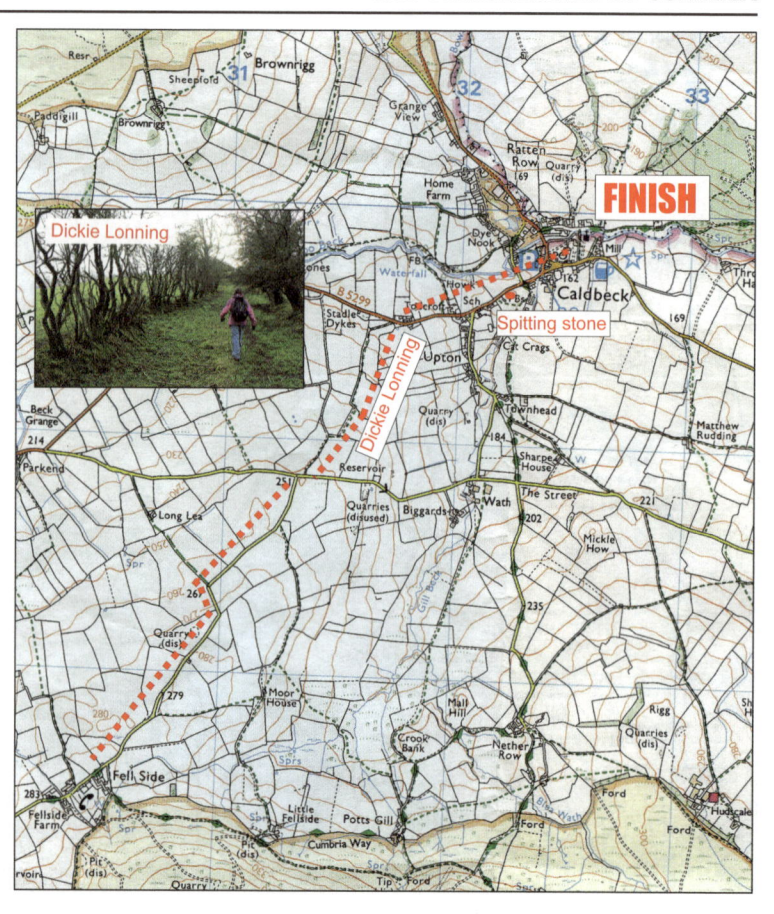

The Bassenthwaite to Caldbeck corpse road follows the Cumbria Way for much of its route

Telling the Bees

One of the more curious customs surrounding death

"The bees, the bees, has anyone told them we're going?"

– Whitehaven mourner, 1820

THE notion that one had to tell the local bees that someone in the house had died seems so strange to us today we searched for as many references as we could – convinced this was some newspaper myth about the naivety of northern rustics. But there are several references to it, in the north of England and throughout other parts of Europe. As late as 1875, the Rev Mr Kemble in his report to the Carlisle Diocesan conference about funeral customs in Cumberland tells how "a singular practice which prevails in certain localities is that of telling the bees of a death in the family, and also turning the hive right round before the corpse is lifted". It must be remembered that in the 18th and 19th Centuries bee hives were an important part of a household's 'livestock' producing its sweet honey so the care of the hives and its residents was considered crucial. And it's clear that a consideration in 'telling the bees' that someone had died would be ensuring they were not distressed to find someone had suddenly vanished, disrupting the status quo and causing stress to the hives.

One of the more detailed references to this custom occurs in a letter written by Dora Harcourt in 1820 to her father Cecil. Dora was staying with relatives near Whitehaven and wrote to her folklore-loving father about the customs and superstitions she came across in Cumberland. During her stay a schoolboy dies and she attends the funeral. She writes:

Telling the Bees included draping the hives with black ribbons

"We had just left the house, when some one whispered, 'The bees, the bees, has anyone told them we're going?' I could not conceive what was meant, and Susanna, to whom the inquiry had been addressed, only said to me, 'Wait for me one moment,' and hastening back a few steps to the sunny wall, where stood the widow's chief wealth, a range of bee-hives, she spoke to them in a tone of singular mournfulness, her words barely audible, they were so interrupted by frequent sobs, as she said, 'Toil on, pretty bees; toil

on, for the widow's sake; but he who loved you best, little Hugh himself, is this day to be carried out a corpse from his mother's house'. I learned afterwards that it was believed the bees would make no more honey if they were not informed when the deceased was going to be buried."

There is also this reference from *The Denham Tracts* (1846 -1859):

"It is still customary to warn the bees of the death of their master, otherwise they will bring luck no longer. One has seen a piece of the funeral cake placed at the mouth of the hive, which the inmates dragged with a mournful noise".

West Cumberland writer William Dickinson noted the exercise of this custom at Asby, near Arlecdon in 1855: *"The superstitious believe that bees* sing the Old Hundredth Psalm on Christmas morning. If one of the family where bees are kept die, one of the household conveys the intelligence to the hives; and on the day of the funeral, before the procession leaves the house, the bees are again informed that the body is about to be lifted. This is believed to prevent ill-luck to the hives and honey." (*A Glossary of Words and Phrases of Cumberland*. William Dickinson, 1859)

In *Old Yarns of English Lakeland* (1914), William T Palmer wrote: "First of all, in these regions of fragrant purple heather, the bees had not to be forgotten. As soon as death had entered the house, some one, generally a woman-body in decent black, went to whisper to the busy workers what had occurred, but the bees did not, as in some places, make the mournful occasion excuse for a holiday. The hives were braided with black – as a child I remember seeing a rusty ribbon on the straw skep and asking the reason – and on the funeral day wine and sweet butter were placed in the orchard or garden for the consolation of the bees."

Fiends Fell

The Cross Fell corpse road – taking on the Helm Wind

"A local legendary tradition ascribes the expulsion of the demons of the storms from the 'fiends fell' to Augustine"

— **Mary Powley, 1875**

ANOTHER 'well known' corpse road is the one from Garrigill to Kirkland which was documented in the late 19th Century by a couple of local antiquarian writers: W. Wallace and Caesar Caine. Vicar Caesar Caine crops up again when he moves to Cleator and details the corpse roads there. And it is his relation, Hall Caine, who popularised the legend of the phantom horse on the Wasdale to Eskdale corpse road.

The path itself is an arduous 16km route from Garrigill to Kirkland in the Eden Valley, reaching a height of 893 metres on the top of Cross Fell. But it's for good reason that Cross Fell is also known as Fiends Fell. This hill takes the worst of the winter storms and it is also home to the only named wind in Britain, The Helm Wind. We have, however, seen references to the 'back wind' at Derwentwater which might also count as a named wind. There is some confusion about the Helm

154 : FIENDS FELL   THE CORPSE ROADS OF CUMBRIA

The Road to Cross Fell, also known as Fiends Fell

Wind but essentially it is a wind which occurs between the larger Helm cloud usually sitting over Cross Fell and a smaller white strip of cloud called the Bar or Bur which sits further west. Here's a description from *The Victoria History of the County of Cumberland* (1901):

"...There is often seen a large, long roll of clouds, the westerly front clearly defined and quite separated from any other cloud on that side; it is at time poised as it were above the mountain, sometimes resting on its top, but most frequently descends a considerable way down its side; this is called the Helm. In opposition to this at a variable distance towards the west is another cloud with its eastern edge as clearly defined as the Helm, and at the same elevation; this is called the Bar or Bur. The space tween the Helm and the Bar is the limit of the wind. The distance between the Helm and the Bar varies as the Bar advances or recedes from the Helm; this is sometimes not more than half a mile, sometimes three or four miles;

"A local legendary tradition ascribes the expulsion of the demons of the storms from the 'fiends fell' to Augustine and his forty followers, who, in the course of their missionary labours in these parts, erected upon the hill in question a cross from which it is said since to have been called Cross Fell.
— *Echoes of old Cumberland, Poems and Translations,* Mary Powley, 1875

occasionally the Bar seems to coincide with the Western horizon, or it disperses and there is no Bar, and then there is a general east wind extending over all the country westward. However violent the wind may be between the Helm and the Bar the violence ends there, as on the west side of the Bar there is either no wind at or, or it blows in the contrary direction..."

Mr W. Wallace's account of the corpse road (also a miners' track) is the earliest we have traced so far from his 1890 book, *Alston Moor: Its pastoral people, its mines and miners, from the earliest periods to recent times*:

"The old people living in Garrigill frequently said that in former times there was a closer connection between the parish of Garrigill and the parish of Kirkland than with the parish of Alston. What this connection consisted in, or how, or when formed, I have never been able to learn with certainty. It is, however, very remarkable that the dead were carried from Garrigill to be interred at Kirkland. I was once informed by Mr Thomas Millican, who was the agent for Messrs Fydell and Tufnell's, Tynehead Manor, that a corpse was taken from Garrigill in the depth of winter to be interred at Kirkland. The funeral party was overtaken with a snow storm, and had to return home to save their lives, leaving the coffin on the top of Cross Fell, where it remained for a fortnight. When the storm subsided they brought the corpse back to Garrigill and buried it in a piece of Glebe Land. The Bishop of Durham having been informed of the circumstance ordered a portion of the Glebe Land to be walled in, and then came to consecrate it for a burial ground. I suppose this occurred about the middle of the seventeenth century or a few years later."

When Rev Caesar Caine, vicar of Garrigill, published his book, *Capella de Gerardegile* or *The Story of a Cumberland Chapelry* (Garrigill), 18 years later he was able to add some more information. Specifically he noted a death on Cross Fell recorded in the register which he thought might have given rise to Wallace's story:

"Two men in the winter time, were once travelling from Garrigill to Kirkland. one suddenly caught sight of a moving mass of ice and snow, and called to his companion.

Further Reading

Capella de Gerardegile or *The Story of a Cumberland Chapelry* (Garrigill) – Caesar Caine

Echoes of old Cumberland, Poems and Translations by Mary Powley (1875):

Alston Moor: Its pastoral people, its mines and miners, from the earliest periods to recent times – W Wallace (1890)

But the alarm came too late! The other was caught by the avalanche and killed. This incident is noted in the Kirkland Register. Is this the origin of the story of the corpse being left on the mountain for a fortnight?!"

And he adds one seemingly unique funereal custom which he says was told to him by people in the parish that "after leaving the Church the corpse was carried three times round the building before being conveyed to the grave".

St John's Church, Garrigill

158 : FIENDS FELL THE CORPSE ROADS OF CUMBRIA

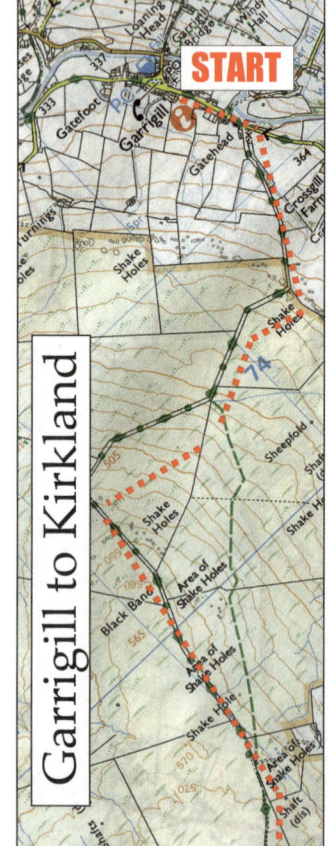

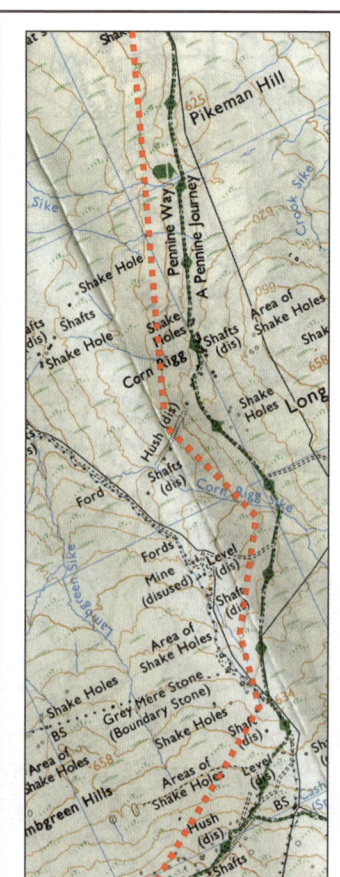

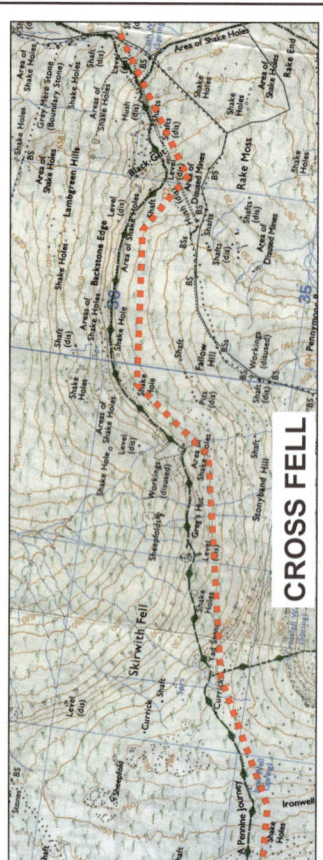

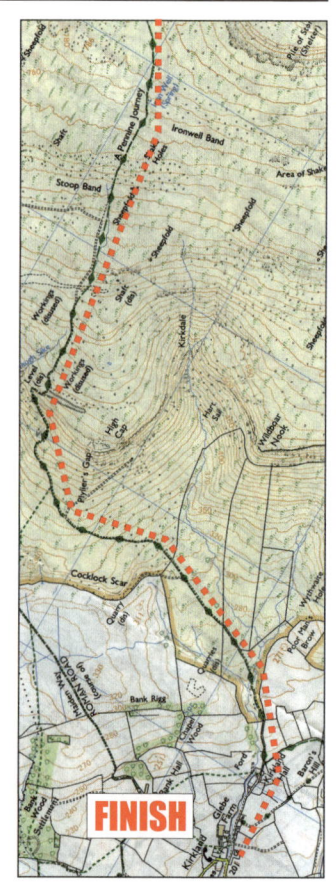

Garrigill to Kirkland

START

CROSS FELL

FINISH

Garrigill to Kirkland

THIS corpse road is a long and arduous walk and takes you to a height of 893m so you'll need appropriate clothing. It can be bright sunshine in the valley below but a blizzard on top of the fells. The walk is really too long for a day-long trek so look to start from either Garrigill or Kirkland and enjoy a walk to the top and a sight of Cross Fell (Fiends Fell) before turning back.

Grade: Tough but the track is well used and easy to follow.

Map: OL 31 – Explorer

Distance: 16.5 km

The Walk: Garrigill is in Cumbria, despite being part of the Pennines. Park in the village and use the opportunity to visit St John's Church – a chapel of ease until it was 'promoted'. There is a public toilet in the village. Nearby Alston also has plenty of cafes and facilities. Head south and at the end of the village you will see a turning to the right signposted Pennine Way. The walk up the fell follows a good single track road but it is of course an uphill climb. You are following the Pennine Way (also called Pennine Journey) marked on OS maps but it skirts the western edge of Cross Fell (previously known as Fiends Fell). If you start from Kirkland, park near the church of St Lawrence the Martyr and head north out of the village onto the fells.

Liggin' kessin'

Liggin' kessin' is a dialect term which literally translate as 'upside down' and it is used to describe sheep who have fallen onto their back. If you see a sheep liggin' kessin' (as pictured above) please help it back up. It can't get back up on its own and will die if not rescued. Just beware that sheep can bite!

You Are Bidden

The custom of bidding mourners to a funeral

"Poorer people sent 'bidders', funereal-looking individuals, who may still be seen going from house to house, generally of an evening"

— **North Country Sketches, Notes, Essays and Reviews. Geo Neasham 1893**

TODAY, details of a funeral are published in the local paper or shared on Facebook and Twitter, sometimes with specific requests such as 'no flowers' but donations to a chosen charity. There's usually a general sense that only close family members have a 'duty' to attend. But in the 18th and 19th Centuries in Cumberland and Westmorland there was a more regulated form of 'bidding' people to a funeral and it seems almost inconceivable that you would refuse such a command. Bidding was normally done verbally, perhaps by a family member or friend but also by a member of the church or parish. And it seems a certain number of people from each part of the parish would be bidden to ensure the community was properly represented. In upper class homes, bidding was also made by a written invitation. An example of the wording of one such invitation is given by George Neasham in 1893 in his *North Country Sketches, Notes, Essays and Reviews*:

"Sir, We are heartily sorry to invite you to Newhall on this dismal occasion, but as It's

a Debt which we all must sooner or later pay, hope you'll honour my Sister and I with your company on Thursday next by 11 o'clock in the forenoon, in order to attend her Husband's Corpse to Lanchester Church and the favour will always be acknowledged by the Family, and, Sir, your most Obedient, Humble Servant, G Whittingham. Newhall, October ye 8th, 1751"

When Dora Harcourt stayed near Whitehaven in 1821, she records a bidding: *"On the day before the funeral the clerk of the village church went round from house to house with a bell, which he rang in a peculiar toll, denoting the parish to which the deceased belonged. Every now and then he stopped, while his long funeral band, placed in his hat, floated on the breeze, as he made proclamation: 'All friends and neighbours are desired to attend the burial of Hugh Johnstone, from Red Hope-lane to St James's Church, tomorrow at three o'clock.' This was the general invitation; but to the dwelling of those most nearly connected, and to the more influential persons in the neighbourhood, there was sent round a young girl wearing a large white calash, and carrying a tray under her arm, in which were laid, neatly folded packets of white paper containing gloves and bands. One set of these articles was left at my uncle's, and on Friday, about noon, the whole family went down to Widow Johnstone's, where preparations for the ceremony had been made on a large scale."*

It is interesting that she draws a distinction between a general invitation and those who were given a specific request to attend.

William Dickinson, a 19th Century antiquarian who also lived near Whitehaven makes a similar point in his book, *A Glossary of Words and Phrases of Cumberland* (1859):
"Next the 'bidding' to the funeral. Often the dale was divided into 'biddings' and I well remember the carpenter-undertaker's apprentice going from farm to farm and cottage to cottage: 'The funeral of [John Thompson] will take place tomorrow [or day after] at three o'clock at the church. To lift at the Haggs at two o'clock. Two from this house are bidden'. In other districts in the case of important persons, three might be bidden from each house in the immediate neighbourhood, two from each house in the next district, and one from each a wider area. It was considered an important duty to be present at every funeral if at all possible, as it was to pay a call at every house where someone was ill."

'Lifting' refers to the moment when the body was lifted from the house onto the bier or the shoulders of the mourners – a moment that had its own specific customs.

Rev Mr Kemble in his summary of funeral traditions in Cumberland in 1875 talks about bidding and says that written invitations are usually sent but at Sebergham there is still "a person who regularly undertakes the duty of bidding" and at Penrith and Carlisle it is usually the Bellman who takes on this duty. He adds, presumably through gritted teeth: *"The practice is to invite all within a certain boundary to attend at the house of the deceased some hours before the time fixed for 'lifting;' and this fashion of inviting a large circle of friends to gather together early in the day furnishes opportunity for the feasting and drinking which, as already observed, not unfrequently results in excess and unpunctuality".*

As to the numbers bidden, this is difficult to ascertain. Keswick's John Richardson wrote in 1876 (*Old Customs and Usages of the Lake District*) that "two were invited from every house in the Laatin… and these with the friends from a distance usually made a pretty large gathering". A Laatin being a part of the parish. And he added: "A substantial dinner was provided for all comers as well as a supply of ale and spirits and tobacco for those who chose to smoke". Manuscripts from 18th Century Troutbeck suggest around 250 were bidden to funerals.

Further Reading

A Westmorland Village; The story of the Old Homesteads and Statesman SH Scott, 1904

Old Customs and Usages of the Lake District By John Richardson (Keswick. Read at Cockermouth and Keswick). Printed 1876

North Country Sketches, Notes, Essays and Reviews. Geo Neasham 1893

Greystoke

One – possibly two – corpse roads to this village near Penrith

"He would not be prevailed upon to permit an hearse to be used, or omit any part of the old ceremonial, and this he expressly commanded before his death"

– Survey of the Lakes, James Clarke 1787

THE 20th Century Cumbrian researcher Jim Taylor Page identified a path leading north from St Andrew's Church, Greystoke as a corpse road saying it led to the hamlet of Johnby. Unfortunately he gives no reference for this assertion but his work is much respected (excepting perhaps his reliance on dowsing for information). *The Story of St Andrew's Greystoke* by Canon David Ellis claims no corpse road but does say, "The field on the north side of the church was for the burial of suicide victims, criminals and mad folk. Normally however funerals entered the church via the north door and left by the south one, the north being associated with darkness and fear, and the south with heavenly light. Weddings

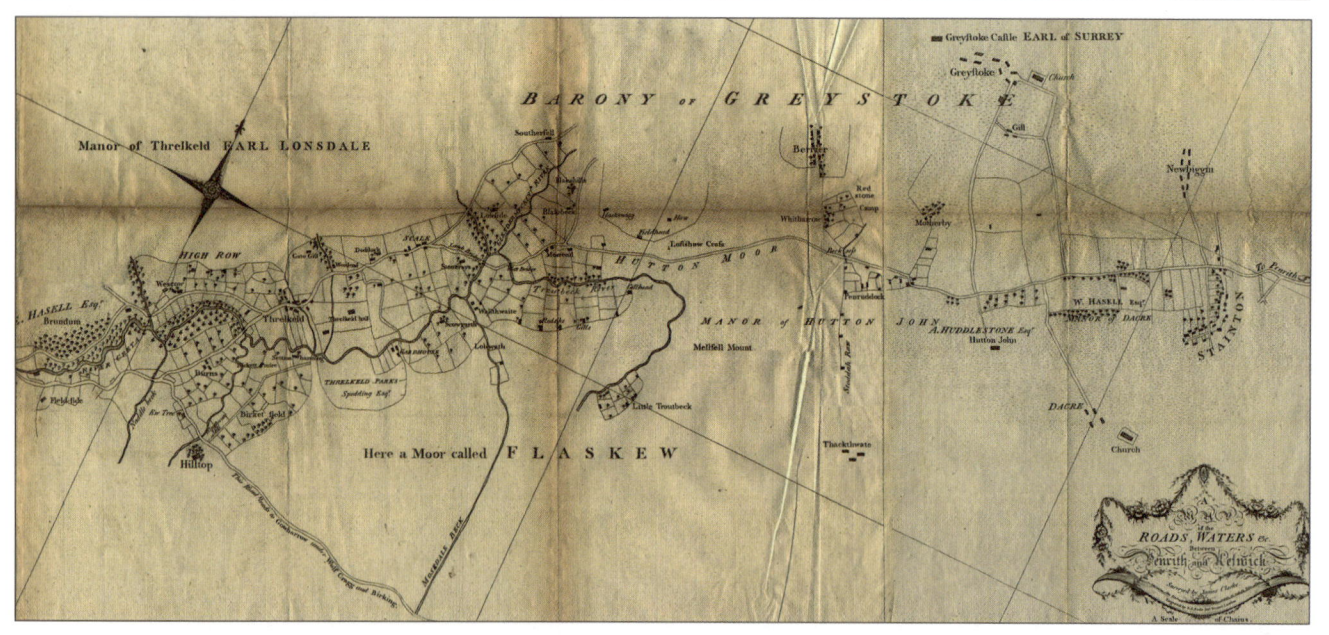

The map of Greystoke from Clarke's *Survey of the Lakes* (1787). He tells of a funeral procession from Lowside to Greystoke.
Src: www.geog.port.ac.uk

reputedly came the opposite way!". This repeats the common church superstitions about the north door (the devil's door) and the north side

of the graveyard. This for instance, from William Wallace's *Alston Moor: Its Pastoral People, Its Mines and Miners, From The Earliest Periods To Recent

Times* published in 1890: "The prejudice against burying the dead on the north side of the church seems to have existed in Garrigill, for the south side is full of graves, none having been made on the north side."

However, a first-hand account of a possible use of a corpse road is given by James Clarke in his *Survey of the Lakes*, published in 1787. He also details funereal customs in this part of the world in the late 18th Century:

"It is worth while here to mention some singular customs in use at funerals in these environs. Notwithstanding some tenements in this dale are seven miles distant from Greystoke, they are all obliged to bury their dead there: all the relations of the deceased who reside within twenty miles, and all the neighbours, attend the funeral. A dinner is provided for them, and after dinner two pennyworth of wheaten bread,

The Spiller's Stone near Greystoke Church. According to legend, coins were left in vinegar in the hole in the top by plague victims for goods; the vinegar cleansing the plague from the coins

and a piece of cheese (by way of viaticum I suppose) is given to each person: the corpse is then laid upon a bier, and carried upon the shoulders of those who attend by turns, (a piece of duty from which even the women are not exempted) till they arrive at a large stone at Greystoke town-head: Here they set the coffin down, and from hence it is carried to the church, (which is distant near a mile) by six persons, upon napkins: during this last part of the procession, the parish-clerk and people sing a psalm before the body, and walk, (be the weather as bad as it will) with their hats off. After the corpse is interred the company retire to the ale-house, here they are again refreshed with bread and cheese, and ale.
This method is invariably followed, whatever be the quality of the

The village of Greystoke. The cross dates from the early 16th Century

deceased; an instance of which I saw about three years ago, when a person of considerable property was thus carried from Lowside, during a very deep snow: scarce any one present had a horse; and though the deceased was much respected, and left no children, (whose property might have been diminished by an expensive funeral,) he would not be prevailed upon to permit an hearse to be used, or omit any part of the old ceremonial, and this he expressly commanded before his death."

Clarke's map of the route (see page 164) cannot be followed precisely today – the A66 cuts through some of it but it is possible to follow it fairly precisely. We have not found yet the "large stone at Greystock town-head" which is described as about a mile from the church but we are hopeful it could be rediscovered. Such large stones were easier to leave where they were than carry off huge distances; at best they were incorporated into dry stone walls or farm buildings.

It is also known that the people in Matterdale took their dead to the mother church of Greystoke. In 1580 they petitioned the Bishop for permission to bury their dead locally rather than be "sore troubled" carrying the dead to Greystoke; the Bishop granted them their request. Older Ordnance Survey maps give a route from St John's in the Vale over Clough Head and Matterdale Common as a corpse road (current maps now calling it an Old Coach Road). But since we know Matterdale

Within sight of Greystoke church is the once famous Eye-keld Well – now in a sadly neglected state

folk took their dead to Greystoke, and the people of St John's in the Vale went to Crosthwaite, this must surely be an error?

There is one other reference we have to a funeral procession to Greystoke which – if only for entertainment purposes – is included.

From *North Country Sketches, Notes, Essays and Reviews by Geo Neasham (1893):* "This mishap in some respects resembles what took place at the burial of the Greystoke miller. He died about the middle of last century, and appears to have been in every respect a second edition of the Elsdon worthy. He loved home-brewed, and was regarded as the best-hearted and jolliest fellow within twenty miles. When a person died at this time, the whole countryside flocked to his funeral, and when the miller was gathered to his fathers, at the ripe age of four-score and ten, it was found that he had left in his will the sum of twenty pounds wherewith to provide meat and drink to all who attended his funeral. Much of both was consumed, it need hardly be remarked, and when the body of the miller was lifted it soon became evident that the mourners had imbibed too freely. The Clerk of Greystoke, who headed the procession, did his best to walk erect, and with a dignity and sedateness of manner befitting the occasion; while the bearers also endeavoured to keep in a straight line with each other and the hearse. The fog of a November evening was falling when the company reached the road leading to

> 'The clerk fell head-foremost into the church, the six bearers following immediately in his wake tumbling pell-mell after him, the coffin falling on the top of them with a crash, and the violent concussion bursting open the sides and revealing the shrouded body of the old miller'

the church; but by some means or other, instead of keeping to the right, they turned to the left and went in the direction of Penrith. They had not gone far till they met old Squire Huddleston, of Hutton John, who, concluding from the unsteady appearance of the mourners that something was wrong, commanded the procession to stop, and inquired if the miller had desired his remains to be carried to market before burial. As may be imagined, there was great dismay among the leaders, each casting the blame on the other for the mistake. Having retraced their steps, the party at length reached the church, but found that the parson, tired of waiting, had gone home. While a messenger went off in search of him, the bearers shouldered the coffin, and preceded by the clerk, prepared to enter the church. Now, it so happened that there were three steps down from the porch, and forgetting this fact, the clerk fell head-foremost into the church, the six bearers following immediately in his wake tumbling pell-mell after him, the coffin falling on the top of them with a crash, and the violent concussion bursting open the sides and revealing the shrouded body of the old miller. The affair created a great sensation at the time, although everybody immediately concerned did his best to hush it up. By common consent, the whole blame was put upon the poor clerk. who is said to have presented a pitiable and humiliating spectacle as he took his place in his little desk the following Sunday morning."

The Sanctuary Stone near Greystoke Church. It has been moved slightly from its original position but apparently marked the boundary at which fleeing suspects could claim sanctuary inside the church grounds

Exit stage left

Leaving home for the last time with dignity intact

"Death is the quiet haven of us all" – **William Wordsworth**

THERE are some practical considerations when it is time to remove the deceased from his or her home and take the corpse on its final journey. One of the more ingenious ideas dreamed up in times gone by was using the frame of the bed as the woodwork for the coffin. Recycling at its best!
We have also come across accounts of older farmhouses having a tradition that one particular door was only used when the corpse of a family member had to be taken out on the way to the funeral.
In St Bees, 500-year-old Crosshill House still retains the 'corpse drop' that was used to enable anyone who died upstairs an easier egress. The house has a narrow spiral staircase which would make removing a corpse rather difficult and undignified so the floorboards were deliberately left loose so they could be removed and the corpse 'dropped' on ropes to the ground floor.
There is also an intriguing reference in *Hawkshead its history, archaeology, industries, folklore, dialect etc*, published in 1899. The author HS Cowper makes mention of 'corpse doors' as an architectural feature in farmhouses in the district. Specifically these were

doors at the rear of the premises but on the first floor. Cowper writes: "Some time ago the father of the present writer was making alterations at a farm at Hawkshead Hill, and in doing so it was found that the door opposite the front door, which we have mentioned in the description of farm-house architecture, was, as is often the case, at the head of a short flight of steps, and had been walled up. One of the workmen, a man long connected with the district, said he had heard that these doors were originally made to take coffins out by. To us this seems very probable. The original idea of these doors on the first floor was partly superstitious - they were the corpse doors, by which the dead were removed, so that the spirit might not find his way in again by the threshold, which was always open. Moreover, the very fact that so many of these doors are now walled up, shows that they were not really necessary, and superstition becoming moribund, the dalesman felt the cold draught and closed them. This may be guesswork, but we do not think it is. In Pembrokeshire it was once the custom to drag the corpse in a shift to the chimney top, and then lower it again. This strange custom has been conjecturally explained as 'purification by fire' rite, but we venture to see in it simply a survival of a time when the dead were hoisted through a hole in the roof, for exactly the same reason which we have suggested the first-floor back doors in our farmhouses were initially made for."

The corpse drop at Crosshill House. The spiral staircase necessitates the removal of the beams should anyone die upstairs

Ling Fell

A short walk with rewarding views towards Cockermouth

"Just above the Lorton Valley, there is a large flat stone. This is known as the old Corpse Stone."

– Jas P Garner 1968

THIS is a corpse road which stops in the middle of nowhere – the top of Ling Fell, near Cockermouth – but is a delightful walk for all that. It may also be the only corpse road to come into existence through a spelling mistake. The first edition of the Ordnance Survey map for the area is the first written record of this corpse road but calls it a "copse road". Later editions of the map were changed to 'corpse road'. Was it ever a corpse road or was it perhaps a road leading to a copse that was then re-interpreted as a spelling mistake? We tend to favour the notion it was at one time a corpse road perhaps connected with the now derelict chapel at nearby Kelsick and leading to Lorton Church. This was the view of a Jas P Garner who described the route in *Cumbria* magazine in October 1968: "The ruins of Wythop

St Cuthbert's Church, Lorton – the possible original destination of the Ling Fell corpse road

old church, situated near Kelsick Farm, and in use until a hundred years ago, when a new church was built on the other side of the fell, had no burial ground attached to it. Lorton churchyard was regarded as the burial ground for Wythop residents. It was therefore customary in those days to take the shortest route, since all corpses were carried by hand, and the Corpse Road would leave the main Wythop Road about quarter a mile past Eskin Farm and reach over Ling Fell in the shortest road to Lorton. As the route travels down Wilson Planting, just above the Lorton Valley, there is a large flat stone. This is known as the old Corpse Stone, since the coffins were rested there if the bearers were rather early for a service." Sadly we have been unable to locate the 'old Corpse

The corpse road skirts round Ling Fell and is easy to pick out

Stone'. Some detailed historical work has been done on Lorton by Ron George of High Lorton (1995) and is available in a pamphlet, *St Cuthbert's Church, Lorton*, from the church. He points out that Lorton was a parochial chapelry belonging to the mother church at Brigham, with the first mention of a 'church' at Lorton being 1198 (and Buttermere in 1198 and Wythop in 1552). Lorton would enter the Diocese of Carlisle in 1883 (becoming a parish in its own right at that time), Wythop becoming a part of the parish of Embleton and Buttermere a separate parish in 1884. Ron George points out there have been burials at Lorton from "the beginning of our parish records – 1538 – and since Lorton was a parochial chapelry, may well have had burials there since it acquired that status". He is sceptical of a corpse road between Wythop and Lorton (and Lorton to Embleton) but points out burials from Buttermere "have always been, and still are, at Lorton". Any corpse road from Buttermere would surely have simply followed the main track/road along the bottom of the Vale of Lorton.

The Old Chapel at Kelsick

If only for romantic purposes rather than historically accurate ones, we start this corpse road from the Old Chapel at Kelsick. This is now a ruin but believed to date back to the 14th Century. A Mr William Alexander who died in 1910 could recall attending the church with his late

The ruins of the former chapel at Kelsick

wife, reporting, "the church was then in a dilapidated condition defected floor, mouldy walls sprouting grass," and adding that, "at one time the bell was suspended from the branch of a tree" (Src: *Binsey Link*, July 2017). We are happy to report, however, that a service is still held at the ruins once a year by the Binsey Mission Community. It is always held on the third Sunday in August at 3pm except in poor weather.

176 : LING FELL						THE CORPSE ROADS OF CUMBRIA

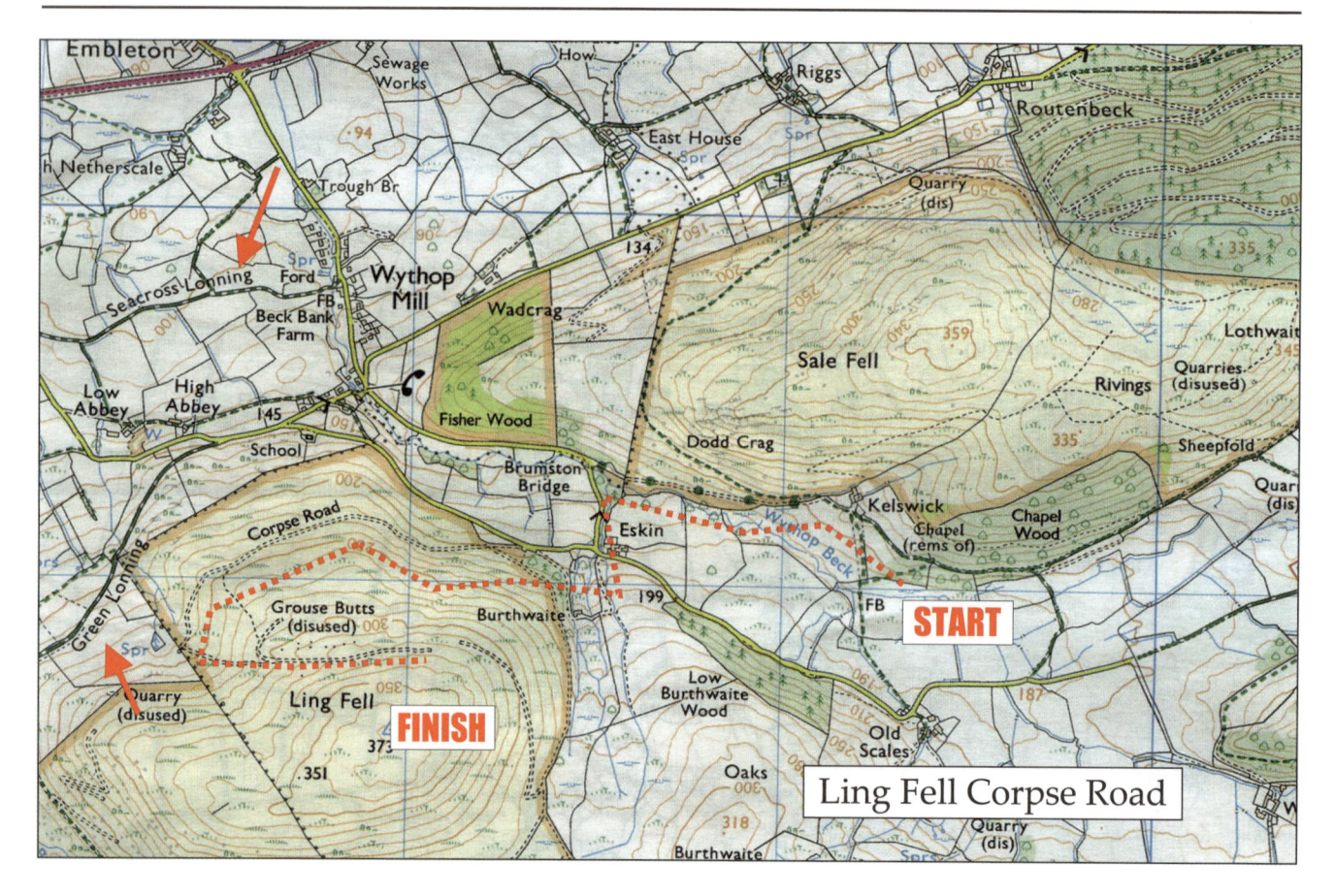

Ling Fell

The Walk: This is a one-way moderate walk. Once you reach the top of Ling Fell you will have to turn round and come back. At the fell boundary before the path turns for the final time near to the top of the fell, you can see the continuation of the corpse road, but it is no longer a public right of way at this point..

Distance: 4.5km

Map: OL 4 – Explorer

Parking: There is parking in unofficial lay-bys.

Refreshments: The Pheasant Inn at Bassenthwaite; this can also be a place to park (in the lane nearby) and walk through to Kelsick chapel and on to the corpse road but this will add about an hour to your walk. There are other pubs and cafes at Embleton and Cockermouth. If you are intending to also visit St Cuthbert's Church, Lorton, you'll also find refreshments there including at The Village Shop (www.lortonvillageshop.co.uk).

Things to see: Nearby you can walk a couple of lonnings: Seacross Lonning and Green Lonning (both on the OS map). Lonnings are a particular type of Cumbrian country lane.

The Walk: We recommend starting with a visit to the former chapel at Kelsick. If you have parked in the lanes under Sale Fell, it will mean

Seacross Lonning, Wythop Mill

doubling back on yourself afterwards but is well worth the short detour. Drop down from the old chapel and walk along the roads past Eskin until you take the path on to Ling Fell. The corpse road/path is usually clearly marked and is well used – not least by the local fell-running fraternity. It's a short walk that ends at the top of the fell. Complete your day with a trip to the church at Lorton.

Coffin rests

A look at the coffin rests and corpse stones still to be found in the landscape

"Come to me, all you who are weary and burdened, and I will give you rest"

— Matthew 11:28

HAND in hand with the corpse roads of Cumbria are the coffin rests, or coffin stones, that can still be found beside some of the paths. They are a mixed selection of small and large boulders which, with the exception of one or two, lie neglected and unmarked. We're also including in this section wayside crosses that lined the corpse roads – and we wouldn't rule out that a number of coffin rests started life as a cross.

So what precisely were coffin rests? With almost no official records of the stones and what they were, we're forced to speculate but we'll start with one 'official' record: the anonymous notice that appears beside the Grasmere 'coffin stone or resting stone' (even the naming of them is not clearly defined) just above Dove Cottage. The sign says: "This stone along with others along the way was used for supporting the coffin while the bearers rested". And that's a common – but modern view

– of their purpose: somewhere to rest the coffin while the bearers had a break. There's little doubt some stones were used that way and a rare first hand account appears in *Devon & Cornwall Notes and Queries* published in 1902 by John S Amery. His account is rather colourful: "The Coffin Stone is so called in consequence of its having long been customary to rest the coffin here, when a corpse is being carried to Widecombe-in-the-Moor for burial. The letters are the initials of some whose remains have here been placed for a while when on the journey to the tomb. I have seen the mourners grouped around this stone, in the quiet stillness of a summer afternoon, while the bearers rested in their toilsome ascent. The blue sky clear and cloudless, the river below laughing in the sunshine, all nature looking bright and joyous, but failing to cheer those hearts saddened and filled with woe."

But this is an explanation which doesn't stand up to examination; not least because of the rather small resting stone at Grasmere. If the bearers were tired, why not just put the coffin on the ground? If it was being carried by horse or cart there would be no need to rest. And would the boulder on which the coffin rested necessarily gain long-lasting fame?

There is, incidentally, a second coffin rest on the Ambleside to Grasmere corpse road (pictured bottom right) – and we are giving grid references for each one). With scant regard for monuments of historical importance, it has been converted into a seat and

Grasmere coffin rest and sign NY343068

Grasmere coffin rest/seat NY358065

now carries a memorial plaque to one who 'loved this view'; a very modern interpretation of 'coffin rest'.

If the Grasmere coffin rest by Dove Cottage is 'too small' then there can be no such complaints about the one on the Nethertown Road at St Bees – though its height may have made it awkward for the mourners to reach. We assume that most of these stones were already there before being used as coffin rests, rather than being brought specially in. WT Palmer writing in the *Newcastle Chronicle* (November 23, 1940) said: "Between Egremont and the church (at St Bees) there is a well defined corpse road over what was formerly unfenced common. At intervals pillars of masonry are built upon which the coffins were deposited while the bearers rested. These pillars are now

The coffin rest on the Nethertown Road, near St Bees NX975101

used as gate-posts, and one of the best examples is on the Ghyll Bottom – Coulderton Road." The corpse road may have been 'well defined' in 1940 but without a map or verbal tradition we can't be sure which route it took. Palmer talks of a number of coffin rests now used as pillars. We can't be sure whether his 'best example' is the one pictured but it is the one today known locally as a coffin rest. If this is one of the original coffin rests then presumably the coffin road came from Egremont and along the Nethertown Road into St Bees. A problem is that St Bees was a major religious institution for centuries and the 'mother church' for much of West Cumbria so almost every path and road into St Bees must have been a corpse road. It is suggestive however that the coffin rest is just a few yards along from Lovers Lonning, an ancient path known previously as Cow Lonning (*Memoirs of John Sewell*, 1852 – 1938). One of the more impressive coffin rests is at Lamplugh (see page 182) and while it is now safely on private land it is against the wall of the main road so easy to see. While it has a tradition of a 'corpse rest' there is not much else that can be said about it. The base has clearly been rebuilt in the past and a post suggestive of it once being a cross stands erect in the centre.

Betty Marshall has done much good work on the history of Lamplugh and has rallied members of the heritage society and other volunteers to her aid. In 2004 she published *Lamplugh Church – Heritage and Traditions of a Cumbrian Parish* and we can do no

> "The use of corpse roads is dying out, if not already dead; all that is known of them being a dim tradition in the minds of the older inhabitants"
>
> – Henry Penfold, 1906

better than quote her section on the village corpse rest:

"The Corpse Rest or Corpse Cross still stands in Lamplugh. The site at one time stood on a strip of common land. It is presently enclosed in a garden, which previously had been a meadow. It stands by the roadside wall that runs between Lamplugh Mill and Low Mill Gill Head. The parishioners of Loweswater certainly used this corpse rest and road, on their way to bury their dead at St Bees. The old corpse road path can still be clearly seen above Holme Wood in Loweswater parish. At the present time a wooden footpath sign near Fangs Brow indicates the route. The next Corpse Cross known on the way to St Bees was at Crosslacon, Frizington (see picture on page 183).

The Lamplugh Corpse Rest

(Grid reference: NY081207)

This does not stand on its original site. It was more of an ecclesiastical design and on the Celtic cross top was a special area to place a book while the priest said prayers. The Lamplugh Corpse Rest is quite plain but functional and has in the centre of a slab of stone, a pillar of sandstone four feet five inches high and nine and a half inches square, partly chamfered on its edges and bearing on its top marks of a sundial plate. The pillar fits the socket hole well. The difference between the workmanship and the rude slab of masonry below is marked. Why should a sundial require such an enormous base or be perched so high it would be necessary to climb up to see the time? The pillar appears to be of a later date than the base."

We share Marshall's scepticism about it being used at one time as a sun dial – at best it was ornamental vandalism. She not unreasonably joins the dots between the corpse road over Loweswater to Lamplugh, on to Frizington and then on to St Bees but most historians would need more evidence before coming to this conclusion. But another piece of the jigsaw is provided by Neil A Burgess in his (undated) *Modern History of St Paul's Church* (Frizington):

"With there being no church at Frizington, there was no burial ground. So when a person died they were either interred at Arlecdon Church or at St Bees Church. The corpse was carried to St Bees by monks from Calder Abbey or by mourners. The route they took to St

The Crosslacon in a private garden at Rheda Park, Frizington NY025167

Bees went along the road from Frizington to Bowthorn and along the road to Hensingham. They would then go along the road to Egremont and cut off near where Bigrigg Church stands today. There are several resting stones on the route, one of which is on the Bowthorn side of East Lodge, Frizington and there is an ancient cross near here which stands on Rheda Estate. The cross formerly stood at Crosslacon. It was moved to its present site by Thomas Dixon. The cross bears the inscription 'Crosslacon' and other than that there is no other inscription on the cross. It is about three and a half feet high. Tradition states that when a corpse was being taken to St Bees the corpse was rested here and a part of the burial service said by one

A stone pillar on the Devil's bridge at Kirkby Lonsdale. It has the inscription 'Feare God, Honer the King, 1673'. It may have been a plague stone or perhaps part of a coffin rest/cross as it is on the corpse road from Killington to Kirkby Lonsdale

of the monks. Part of the cross top is broken off which is what the book would be rested on. It bears the name Fallen Cross. It may have been a boundary cross."

The survival of the roadside cross at Crosslacon (now moved to a private garden) helps us to a more likely conclusion: Some coffin rests were not a place for weary pall bearers to rest the coffin and catch their breath. They were stations at which the procession paused for the singing of a hymn or uttering of a prayer. This is supported by numerous accounts of funeral processions in the 19th Century stopping at specific points for just such a purpose. Hence Whellan's *History of Cumberland* published in 1847 says: "Two stone crosses, called Corpse Crosses, formerly stood on the common (at Castle Sowerby), and it is stated that when a body was being carried to the parish church for interment, it was usually set down here while a prayer was said for the repose of the soul of the deceased."

The Castle Sowerby crosses are now lost.

Dorothy Wordsworth records in her journal (3rd September 1800): "They set the corpse down at the door and while we stood within the threshold the men with their hats off sang with decent and solemn countenances a verse of a funeral psalm. The corpse was then borne down the hill and they sang till they had got past the Town-end… When we came to the bridge they began to sing again and stopped during four lines before they entered the churchyard" (*The Grasmere Journals*).

And from WT Palmer in 1914 writing in the *Liverpool Daily Post* about Cumberland funeral customs: "On the boundary of every township small parties are waiting for the coming of the funeral; some of the very aged struggle down to the roadside to watch yet another passing on 'the long journey', others join in the sad procession. At the nearest halting-place to the church the clerk and singers were wont to meet the cortege. This halting place usually had the name of Cross or Crosses, for it was often the last and first point at which the parish church in the bottom of the glen was visible. And at a slow pace, singing the

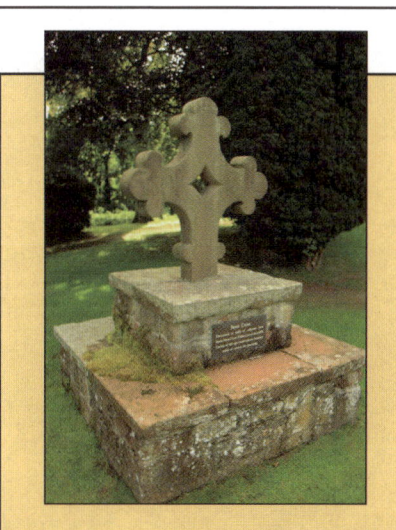

The Fawn Cross now safely in the grounds of the Ennerdale Hotel, Cleator. It originally stood beside Jacktrees Road and may have been on the route of a corpse road to St Bees. It is thought Fawn Cross may have been a corruption of "fallen cross".

The Weeping Cross – previously on the Whitehaven corpse road at NX975134 but now at St Bees Priory NX968120

quaint funeral hymns, the procession moved on, now in proper order, relatives nearest, down the last possible connect, then the friends, in order of age and not of importance. The stonebreaker might precede the squire and no one be a bit the worse. The clergy met the corpse at the lych-gate and then the beautiful service for interring the dead was recited."

Mr Palmer suggests the resting places were the boundaries of townships and this idea is also recalled by Mary Armitt in 1912 (*The Church of Grasmere*). She conjures up an almost romantic image of worshippers wending their way over the fells towards Grasmere and meeting up at certain known points and then "the united groups would travel by the lake, and past the Holy Well, to enter the church garth by a gate at the north-west angle, now gone, called the Langdale gate".

This seems to make more sense of the idea of coffin rests. Different parishes meeting up would need a known meeting place and some wayside cross or named stone beside the path would be ideal. It asks the question whether the How Stone at Grasmere was a more likely 'coffin rest' and meeting place than the insignificant stone currently honoured. Some of these crosses appear to have had their own name and mystique. We have already mentioned the Crosslacon with its 'bible rest' (more likely just a space left by a broken arch of the cross). There is also the Weeping Cross which once stood on the Whitehaven to St Bees corpse road at the point of the former St Michael chapel

(NX975134) and near to St Bega's holy well (in the woods in the valley). It is now safely looked after at St Bees Priory and can be found just outside the main door. Historian Caesar Caine said this about it in *The History of the Rural Churches of the Rural Deanery of Whitehaven* (1916):

"The tympanum on which is sculptured George and the Dragon, used to be spoken of as Viking but from the dress of the mailed figure it is clearly Norman. It is supposed to have been brought from a chapel which once stood at Rottington. The cross once stood midway between St Bees and Whitehaven by the roadside. Here funeral parties rested on their way to the churchyard at St Bees. From this fact is obtained the name of 'weeping cross'."

It's a lovely name and one wonders about other place names such as Sorrowstones near Irton and whether these were once the spots of coffin rests.

Gosforth historian Dr C A Parker was convinced that the location of roadside crosses persisted through place names involving 'cross' and, based on this theory, linked many of them together to create elaborate but little-evidenced corpse roads. In 1907 he recorded the rediscovery of Fawn Cross which is now kept safe in the grounds of the Ennerdale Country House Hotel at Cleator (NY017137). See picture on page 185.

He wrote (in 1907): *"On the Jacktrees road, between Cleator and Cleator Moor, and near the south level crossing, there*

This is known locally as a 'coffin rest'. It is on the banks of the River Ehen at Egremont. A more unlikely 'coffin rest' we are yet to see! NY011101

formerly stood a farmhouse called Fawn Cross, which collapsed some thirty years ago owing to the subsidence of the ground. The late Mr. Ainsworth of the Flosh, thinking that the name was a corruption of 'Fallen Cross,' had excavation made by the roadside and discovered a cross head, which is now upside down on a pedestal in the garden of the Flosh (now the Ennerdale Hotel). It is of red sandstone, cut with a broad chisel, and of good workmanship. The head is free, measuring 19½ inches across the arms, all three limbs expanding slightly and chamfered on their edges, with a small cockspur at the outer end of each chamfer. The ends are plain, flat, and unchamfered, and the intersection of the arms is filled by a plain shield in relief on one of the faces. The shaft is broken short off, and might well be restored."

Dr Parker suggest the original site of the Fawn Cross (on Jacktrees Road) was part of a corpse road that led eventually to St Bees. His logic runs: "From Fawn Cross the road runs through Cleator to Pallaflat, in the parish of Egremont, where it passes Coltmoor Cross and Jordan's Cross, and then runs on to Loughrigg Cross (22 miles in all). Here it makes a detour to avoid a steep descent, but a footpath, probably an old corpse road, carries it on in a direct line to the village of St Bees."

But with no other evidence than place names including the word 'Cross' we cannot share his conclusion.

Further reading

The Gosforth District by Dr C A Parker,

Cleator and Cleator Moor Past and Present by Caesar Caine. Reprinted by Michael Moon in 1973

Cleator Moor Revealed – An Illustrated History by Tom Duffy, 2003.

Guide to the Lakes – www.lakesguides.co.uk

Arval Bread & Funeral Feasts

Giving the deceased a good send off with food and drink

"Ivverbody sits down to plenty o' food, wid rum butter and funeral biscuits, and plenty to drink"

– A Gosforth resident in 1956

I DON'T mind going if a lunch is provided – so says one of Scrooge's mourners in Dickens' *A Christmas Carol*. And it's certainly true that even the best of friends expect something to eat or drink at a funeral wake. What food or drink you should receive at a funeral has varied over the years. In Cumberland and Westmorland arval (or arvel) bread was traditionally the funeral fare. William Rollinson defines arval (*The Cumbrian Dictionary*, 1997) as "a small bun, always made of the best wheat flour, which was given to each mourner at the graveside. This was taken home to be eaten in the mourner's house. In some areas arval cheese and arval ale were also distributed in the same manner". It was discourteous to eat the bread there and then; this was something akin to being given today a piece of birthday cake wrapped in a napkin –

something to take away with you to eat. The origin of the word 'arval' is unclear.

The type of funeral fare has varied over the centuries but the distribution of arval bread is probably still within living memory. Bertram Puckle, writing in 1902 in *Funeral Customs*, noted: "in Cumberland, the mourners are each presented with a piece of rich cake, wrapped in white paper and sealed, a ceremony which takes place before the 'lifting of the corpse', when each visitor selects his packet and carries it home with him unopened." If this was not true arval bread it was the late 19th Century equivalent.

Arval is a term used in Cumbria for different aspects of the funeral and

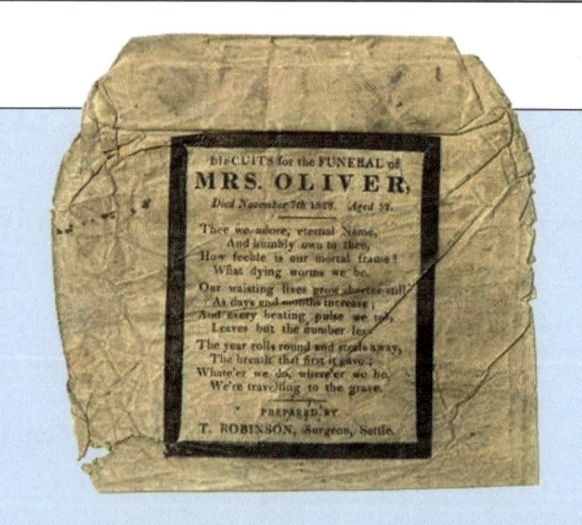

A funeral biscuit wrapper. The words read:

Biscuits for the funeral of Mrs Oliver,
Died November 7th 1878. Aged 52
Thee we adore, eternal Name,
And humbly own to thee,
How feeble is our mortal frame!
Why dying worms we be,

Our waisting lives grow shorter still
As days and months increase;
And every beating pulse we tol,
Leaves but the number less

The year rolls round and steals away,
The breath that first it gave;
Whate'er we do, where'er we be,
We're travelling to the grave.

'the arval' would refer to the funeral tea in all its forms. Hence John Fell spoke at Seascale in 1884 about Dalton in Furness and said: *"In Dalton the custom of the arvel was for the persons attending a funeral to divide themselves into parties of four each. The parish clerk having given notice in the churchyard at what hour and place the arvel would be given, the guests then assembled in their respective parties, a cake of the same description as that known now as a fair cake, but called the arvel cake, was given to each person, and a quart of ale was provided for the four. It was however by custom incumbent upon each part at the arvel festival to order another quart of ale to be paid for by the four to recompense the innkeeper for the use of the room, fire, or stabling provided for the convenience of the mourners or guest at the funeral."*

Cumberland rum butter. For a recipe see soozintheshed.blogspot.co.uk.

Another funeral custom were the 'funeral biskies' – large teacakes made with butter, yeast, sugar, salt and flour. As our picture on page 182 shows, these were made commercially in the latter part of the 19th Century. Rum butter, a West Cumbrian delicacy was served at funerals as it was at baptisms (and still is), weddings and other major life events. It would normally be served with a biscuit or wafer. There is a distinct difference between Westmorland Rum Butter and Cumberland rum butter – Westmorland Rum Butter requires the butter to be creamed into the sugar while the Cumberland variant has the butter melted first. Woe betide any entrant in the county's agricultural shows getting their recipes mixed up!

There were traditional times for specific food and drink. A wake held a day or two after the person's death, a tot of whisky or rum for those lifting the coffin and the arval bread or biskies for the mourners, and a more substantive funeral tea, usually after the funeral.

A Gosforth resident, quoted in dialect, in 1956 described the scene in his day: *"Then all t'folk lines up behind t'coffin, and most of 'em is wearing a bowler hats: to see some on 'em you'd think they'd just come out o't'Hark. They all walks to t'Church, and after service and such they all goes to t'Globe for a funeral tea. Funeral teas is very like weddings. Ivverbody sits down to plenty o'food, wid rum butter and funeral biscuits, and plenty to drink, and most o' t'folks' friends and relations is, maister, t'ad best wait on e'm being buried"*. The same source – *The Sociology of An English Village* – also describes how drink could sometimes interfere with the solemnity of the occasion such as when "a funeral procession which paused at the Wellington Inn for refreshment after a journey from a distant farm, and continued to the Church where it was discovered that the coffin had been left behind on a wall near the public house".

Drink also played its part in another incident in Cleator Moor in the early part of the 20th Century and is recalled by John W Skelly in his book, *Back to the 1920s*: "The holding of 'wakes' on the night before the funeral had not totally died out at that time. On such an occasion friends, and relatives gathered in the home of the deceased. Usually (for some of them) after they had spent the evening in the 'local'. I was present at one of these with my father and one would never have thought that the home was a house of 'mourning'. The singing, the laughter, the joking was altogether contrary to the occasion, and this would go on until five or six in the morning. At this time, in the early hours of the day all, except the members of the household would disperse, perhaps to get a little sleep depending on the arranged time of the funeral. Any mothers that might have been present would of course have to prepare their children for school. It was at this time that I learned of a similar occasion at Cleator Moor not long before, when the corpse was taken out of the coffin and stood up in a corner whilst the merriment was going on. He was an 'uninterested' onlooker."

The church had its views on drink of course and has at times tried to curb the amount of drinking surrounding funerals. It recognised food and drink was a necessity for those who had spent a long time getting to church and attending the funeral but warned against excess. In particular, the 'tradition' of announcing at the graveside which Inn the funeral tea would be held in was frowned upon. And in a surprisingly precognitive sign of today's anti-smoking society, smoking was discouraged during funerals.

It would appear that the custom of a lavish funeral tea or dinner dwindled

'All friends and relations of the deceased are hereby invited to proceed forthwith to the Red Dragon Inn (or whatever was the place of the banquet), there to partake of such refreshment as shall be found provided'

– Alexander Pearson describing the wording of the graveside bidding to the funeral tea in *Annals of Kirkby Lonsdale*, 1930

in the 20th Century. What had started as a tradition of a simple treat of arval bread to the poor had grown into a 'Beating the Joneses' feast but the tradition was now turning full circle. By 1914 WT Palmer was complaining "All the one-time dainties with the exception of sweet butter have gone into the limbo of past things, and the funeral feast has lost much of its character". Instead mourners were introduced to the more frugal 'knife and fork' tea at which they could expect, according to Betty Marshall in her history of Lamplugh, a home cured Cumberland Ham tea – "Cold boiled ham with salads, home baked funeral biskies and cakes were order of the day".

Today the tradition is very much for a cold buffet only with most funeral tea venues offering a simple selection of sandwiches, pork pie, scotch egg, cakes and the like. The Waverley Hotel, in Whitehaven, for example offers soup, ham, tuna mayonnaise and egg mayonnaise sandwiches, meat & potato pie, sausage roll, an assortment of homemade cakes and pastries, and – something to gladden any Cumbrian's heart – scones served with rum butter.

And the start of the 21st Century has seen the arrival of a whole new funeral tradition: the review of the funeral tea on tripadvisor.co.uk. Here's one less than impressed reviewer of a Cumbrian funeral tea. We leave the venue anonymous: *"Although the setting was impressive I must say the afternoon tea provided was unsatisfactory. The tea was placed in the middle of the table and guests left to look after themselves. There were no plates provided we were told 'We don't do plates, napkins are sufficient'. Not good enough. Immediate family (wife of deceased and 2 daughters) had to leave early due to ill health of one of the daughters and requested that a few of the sandwiches be boxed to take with them but were refused the person saying 'We don't do takeaways'. This has never happened to us before with afternoon teas and at a cost of over £20 a head for the tea quite unbelievable. The person spoken to regarding this was quite rude."*

- Note: Biskies were ham (or cheese) served in a sweet bread roll; a similar word but quite different to biscuits.

Further reading

Lamplugh Church by Betty Marshall, 2004

The Parish of Lamplugh – edited by Ann Lister & Betty Marshall, 1993

Funeral Customs – Bertram S Puckle, 1926

Around Brampton

Almost lost corpse roads

"If a funeral is brought to the church by any other way than the orthodox corpse road, the house from which the funeral has come will be again visited by the reaper within a very short time."

– Notes and Queries, 1907

THE corpse road at Hayton has a certain charm but the lack of a definitive footpath as it crosses open fields robs it of any sense of history. Just occasionally there is a return to an enclosed lonning which evokes a charm of its own – otherwise it is open fields, albeit with stunning views across the vale to Carlisle and the Solway. The path directly beside the church and lychgate is the most picturesque part. Holly trees abound here and photographers or artists may wish to wait for a winter's evening when snow is falling to make their visit.

Our reference to this corpse road appears in *Northern Notes and Queries* for 1907, written by Henry Penfold:

"The burial road in Hayton parish went by public road from Fenton village to the How, thence through the fields to Hayton church. What remains of this old path is still

known as the 'Kirk Trods'. The path in Hayton parish was very much broken up by the construction of the Newcastle and Carlisle railway about sixty years ago, though there is still living at the How an old man who perfectly recollects the time when it was in constant use for burial purposes."

Penfold's account includes other corpse roads in the Brampton area but to begin we have chosen the Hayton one as it offers breathtaking views across to Carlisle.

The corpse road at the point in reaches St Mary Magdalene, Hayton

BRAMPTON : 197

Fenton to Hayton

This is a short, pleasant walk which offers grand views to the Solway.

Distance: 2km
Map: OL 315 – Explorer
Grade: Easy

The walk: Park in the village of Fenton (or in Hayton and do the route in reverse). There's no specific parking so park considerately. The route is easy to follow.

Refreshments: The Hayton Farm tea room is just off the A69 and serves lunches, teas, ice creams etc. Brampton also has many cafes and pubs if you want to continue and do the Old Brampton church corpse road.

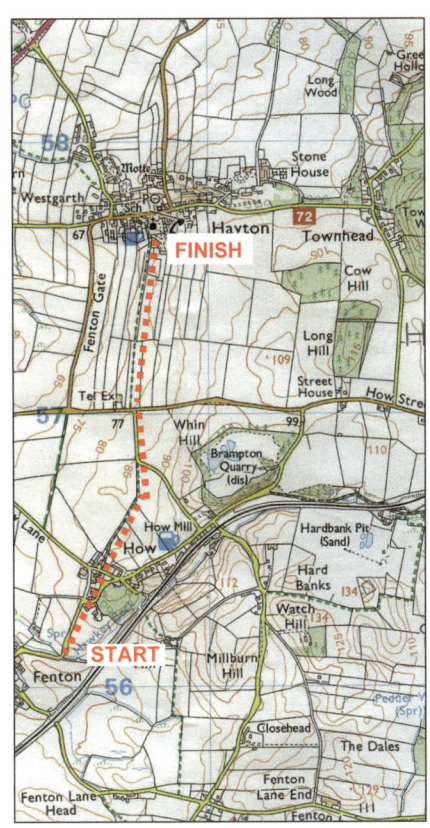

The Hayton corpse road

Mr Penfold details three other corpse roads – or remains of them – in the 1907 *Notes & Queries* article.

Brampton: The current St Martin's Church in the town centre was consecrated in 1878. Prior to that the old church (a couple miles west of the town) was used and it is to this that Mr Penfold's corpse road led. As there is only one road to the church (Old Church Lane) it is safe to assume this was the corpse road. However he also talks about Brampton's Front Street, saying "people going to some inconvenience to take their deceased friends to their last resting place by the road which had been consecrated by long and uninterrupted use".

The road to Brampton old church is a good single track road; in fact it goes to the new cemetery so is in effect still a corpse road! It's easy to find from the town centre. There is a 'short cut' along a footpath but we've been unable to ascertain so far if this path is the ancient route – it's more likely to have been the main road.

Brampton old church – now redundant but a good spot for a picnic

The old church is no longer used but you can obtain a key from the neighbouring farm house if you want to look round. However, just sitting in the old graveyard is a nice spot for a bit of lunch

Stapleton: This corpse road was used to carry the body of any parishioner who died in the part of the parish between Stapleton and Bewcastle to the church at Stapleton (the current church only dates from 1830 but is on the site of an older one) but, importantly, via Longrigg. The Longrigg detour added half a mile but Penfold tells of the superstition which insisted upon its use: "A superstition of a very remarkable character is also connected with this road. If a funeral is brought to the church by any other way than the orthodox corpse road, the house from which the funeral has come will be again visited by the reaper within a very short time. The truth of this interesting legend is proved by many stories, all of the same character, which are told to convince the unbelieving. One of these stories I now give: Some few years ago a death took place in that part of Stapleton parish to which I have already referred. On the appointed day of burial the father of

St Mary's, Stapleton: Destination for the Bewcastle corpse road; an older church once stood on this site. Picture by geograph.org.uk. Rose and Trev Clough

the deceased directed that his son should be conveyed to the churchyard, not by way of the Longrigg, but by the shortest and most convenient route. The older inhabitants were staggered at this unwonted indifference to ancient custom, and prophesied dire results as a punishment for such terrible audacity. Wonderful to relate, the stories came true, and the unfortunate father within a month was on his way to the churchyard on the same mournful mission, and again he was minded to contemptuously break the 'charm' by going the nearer and newer route. When the funeral came to the road end, according to the arrangements already made by the unabashed father, the procession was to pass over the newer way. A dramatic incident here occurred. One of those ancient characters which belong to and adorn every parish was looking out, and on seeing that the old custom, hallowed almost into a duty, was again to be violated, he rushed out and, frantically seizing the bridle of the horse in the hearse, led it into the old and safe way, at the same time admonishing the bereaved father in strident tones for his culpable indifference to a warning which seemed to him nothing less than divine."

We cannot be sure of the route from Bewcastle but the path still exists from Longrigg to Stapleton.

> And what is death?
> Is still the cause unfound?
> That dark mysterious name of horrid sound?
> A long and lingering sleep the weary crave
>
> — John Clare

The Laversdale to Irthington corpse road near Hurtleton

Irthington

The corpse road led from Laversdale to Irthington over land known locally as the 'Scroggs' and past a farm at Hurtleton. Mr Penfold adds that another informant said there was also a corpse road from the hamlet of Old Wall to meet the Laversdale corpse road. This was walled in and called the Roman Walk. It is still a public path and worthy of a slight detour. Interestingly he quotes a correspondent as saying, "My husband says it is forty-five years, as far as he can remember, since a corpse was carried through this way, and my brother-in-law was one of the party who helped to carry …. My husband also remembers a wedding party walking this same way in 1856".

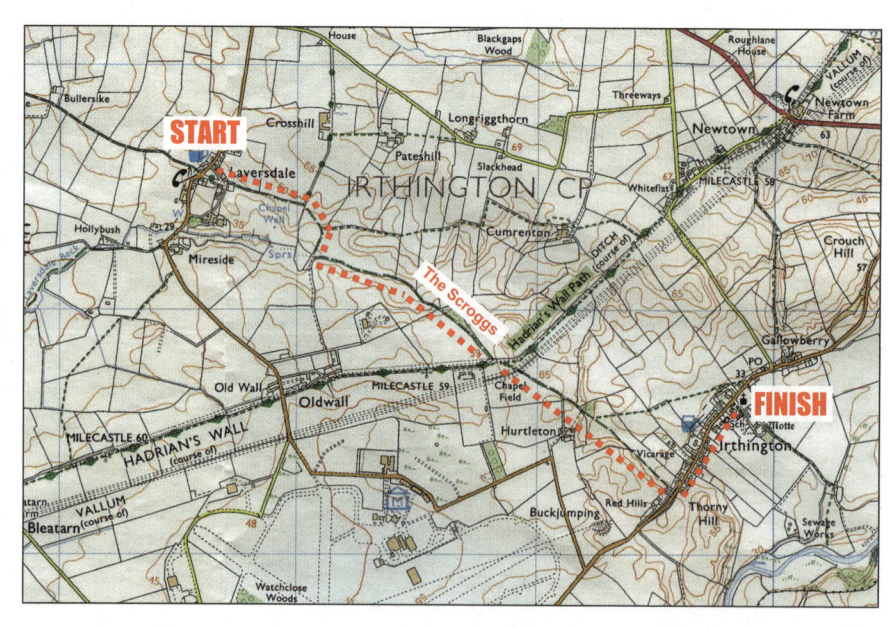

This seems to echo the Irton testimony which talked of corpse roads also being bridal (not bridle) paths.

Grade: Easy

Distance: 3.5km
Map: OL 315 – Explorer
The Walk: Park at Laversdale and head east out of the village between houses and onto the footpath. The first part is quite open but the

landscape suggests that at one point this part of the path may have been hedged in and more of a lonning than it is today. A Chapel Well (spring) is marked on the Ordnance Survey map at the bottom of the slope. As you head into the next field drop down and follow the pylons to the stile on the opposite corner. Go over the stile and the path takes you through the Scroggs (a scrap piece of woodland) to a junction with the Hadrian's Wall path. We recommend taking the detour (south-west) on the path to Oldwall which is recorded by Penfold as once also being a corpse road. When you reach the main road turn back and return to the junction. From the junction follow the path south-east past Hurtleton farm. The path drops down through a pleasant piece of woodland and skirts round a hill before passing through houses into the village of Irthington (there is another footpath marked on the OS map heading more directly to the church but we could not find this). Follow the main road to St Kentigern's church. It was originally built in the 12th Century. The church website says "Our doors are wide open" but sadly we found them locked. St Kentigern is one of Cumbria's very own saints, usually known by his other name, St Mungo.

The other corpse road to Oldwall

A way with the fairies

A corpse road protected by the gentle folk

"The fault of the present age is, not that it believes too much, but that it believes too little. Its illuminati have rejected from their creeds, not only the fables of giants, fairies and necromancers, but the truths of revelation, and the facts of sacred history"

– **Robert Anderson, 1805**

THIS corpse road is detailed in Paul Devereux's *Spirit Roads*, having been gleaned from *Walks In Mysterious South Lakeland* (1997) by Graham Dugdale. But it has a longer tradition than that. Elizabeth Bassett, for example, wrote in *Cumbria Magazine* in 1961 about the church path and its association with the fairy steps at Beetham: "On old maps of this route, adorned on its highest by the so-called Fairy Steps, is marked as Church Walk. Local legend had it, in my young days, that this was the way over the sands to Beetham Church in the days before Witherslack Church was built, and, there was nowhere to bury the dead but in Beetham Churchyard. To carry a corpse through those very narrow ways between the rocks must have been quite a feat. But bearing in mind that our medieval ancestors were smaller than ourselves and the fact that the burial was not in coffins but in shrouds, it might not be so difficult after all, and the bearers could, at the narrowest part, carry the corpse above their heads." Other writers refer to the holes for hooks at

Rain seems to add to the magical quality of the light and scene at Beetham's Fairy Steps

the steps though one is forced to wonder why they didn't just walk round the escarpment.

This path starts at Arnside where the River Kent enters Morecambe Bay but we have also seen references to a corpse road from Witherslack in the north to Beetham. This would have had to cross the treacherous paths over the Kent or the bay – apparently at St John's Cross which is close to the village of Sandside on the south bank of the River Kent. A history of the area (Storth) published in 1956 made this comment:

"It has been found difficult to account for St. John's Cross. Funeral parties, on their way to Beetham may well have forded the estuary here, at some far distant time, and would probably halt at St. John's Cross for

A Brownie Is Not A Fairy

AT the hamlet of Overthwaite is a legendary creature called 'The Tawney Boy'. It was a Brownie, rather than a fairy as the Rev William Hutton was anxious to point out in his work, *The Beetham Repository*, written in 1770: *"A Brownie is not a Fairy, but a tawney colour'd Being which will do a great deal of work for a Family, if used well. We have a story of one, and the only one that I have heard of in this country, living for some time at Overthwaite, in my Great Grand Father's time, about the Year 1650. 'The Tawney Boy' would have done a great deal of work, but after staying six months they clipp'd the hair of it, and gave it a new suit of clothes. On Saturday Night after Dark it went out and was heard to say to somebody, "Daddy they clypp'd me, and pow'd me, and made me bare: But Daddy I am weel and feel nane sare (or sore)." After this the Browneie was never seen more."* This type of creature was known in Cumberland as a hob-thross and there is a famous legend of one that lived at Millom Castle.

rest and refreshment. It is said that they used to kneel here to give thanks for safe arrival after what must have been, at times, a difficult and dangerous crossing. It seems likely that a cross stood here at one time and also that it had some connection with the old Saxon chapel of St. John's at Beetham. This chapel stood near the River Bela, a few hundred yards south-east of where St Michael's now stands. That it had a burial ground is evident from the great quantity of bones dug up on the site many years ago. There was another St. John's Cross which stood between the chapel and the river. Little more is known of this old chapel beyond the fact that it fell to ruin about nine hundred years ago. It is known that the dead were, for many years, brought over from Witherslack to Beetham for burial at St. Michael's, but in this case, the crossing would probably be made by ford or boat from Foulshaw to the Dixies at Sandside.

St Michael's and All Angels Church at Beetham. The largely Victorian church stands on the site of an earlier construction

Such interments went on until about 1669 when Witherslack obtained its own church burial ground, thus bringing to an end the need for any crossing of the river."

We would strongly advise against attempting to cross the Kent or Morecambe Bay. These are treacherous waters and lives have been lost by those unaware of the speed of the incoming tide or the quicksand that will grip you like fast-setting concrete. Since 1548 there has been a Queen's Guide to the Sands to guide people across the bay. The arrival of the railway and motorcar has however reduced the need for this post. The current holder is Michael Wilson who regularly leads walks, usually organised by charities as a fund-raising venture.

208 : BEETHAM

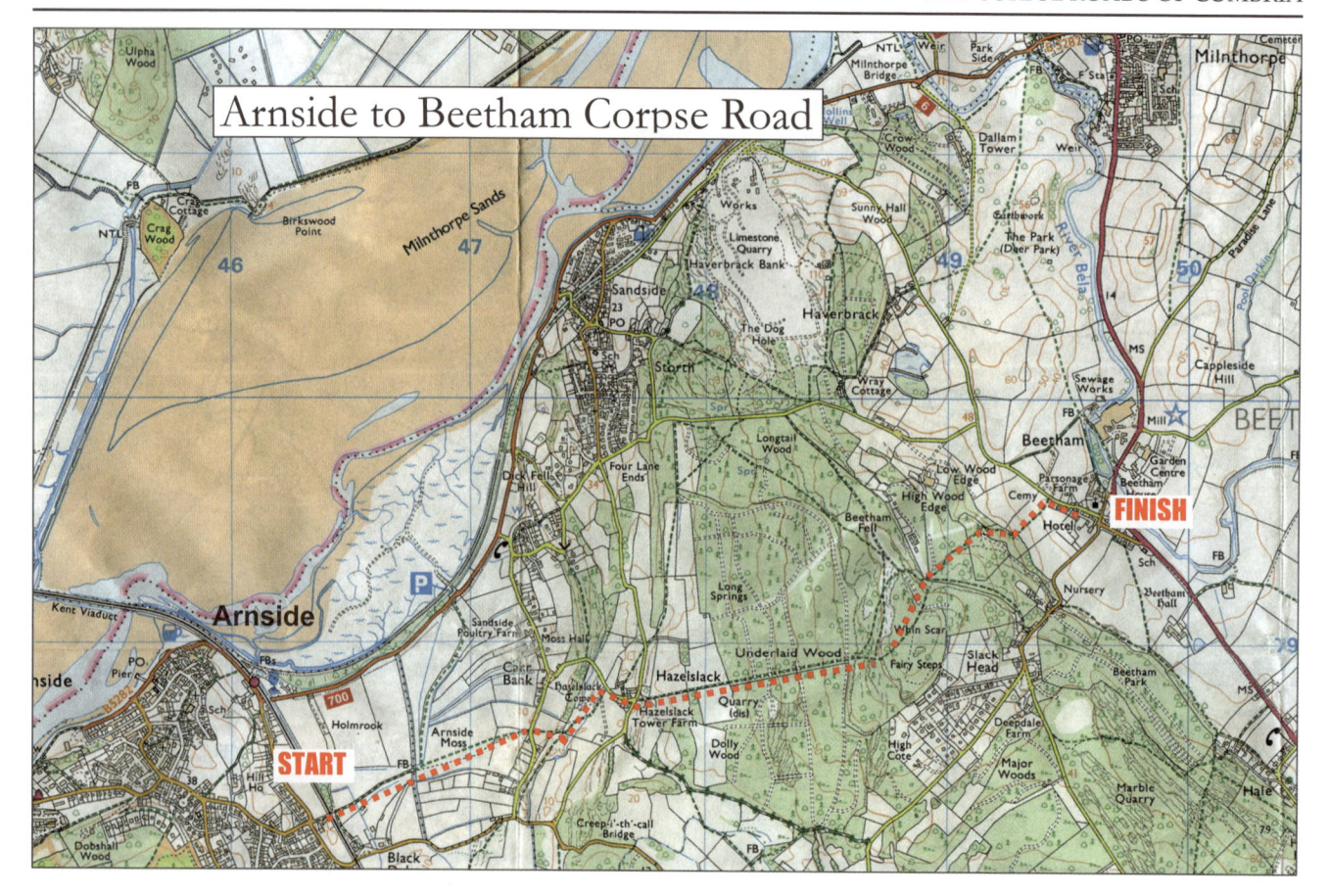

THE CORPSE ROADS OF CUMBRIA

Arnside to Beetham Corpse Road

Arnside to Beetham

A bracing walk taking in the estuary coast, wooded lanes and an archetypal English village

Grade: Easy

Map: OL7 – Explorer

Distance: 4km

The Walk: Parking is relatively easy at Arnside as it caters for the daytrippers spending a day on the estuary coast. The path is easy to follow and is signposted 'Fairy Steps'. Start by walking along Black Dyke Road out of Arnside. Opposite the Briery Bank junction you turn north-east along a well-made path signposted to Black Dyke. After half a mile, select the footpath which will take you past the ruins of the 14th Century pele tower, Hazelslack Tower. This is on private property but is easily visible form the public paths. It's an impressive ruin. Paul Devereux says, *"Hazelslack was previously known as Helslack; 'slack' is an old term for gully or ravine, while 'hel' could have been a reference to the corpse road – for instance, a corpse road in Yorkshire was known as the Old Hell Way."* You will

The path dropping down into the village of Beetham

also notice on the Ordnance Survey map the curiously named Creep-i'-th'-call Bridge. This bridge is on the border of Cumbria and Lancashire. The origin of its name is unclear.

Pass through Hazelslack Tower Farm on to the footpath through Underlaid Wood. Halfway through you will come across the Fairy Steps – try to pass through without touching the sides to be granted your wish from the fairies! Continue through the wood and you will gradually drop down towards Beetham. Cross the final field towards the village and turn right towards the church. One particularly charming feature is the rose pergola which leads to the church.

Refreshments: The Old Post Office tea room opposite Beetham Church has to be one of the nicest in the county. Highly recommended. You'll also find plenty of cafes at the start of the walk at Arnside.

The fairies of Cumbria

CUMBRIA has a surprisingly rich tradition of fairy folk. It includes the tale of the Luck of Eden Hall – a beautifully-decorated glass beaker (pictured). Legend tells that the butler of Eden Hall saw fairies dancing at nearby St Cuthbert's well when he was fetching water. The beaker was in their midst and he snatched it from them. The fairies cried out: "If this cup should break or fall,

Farewell the Luck of Eden Hall". Fortunately, the Luck still survives and is now held by the Victoria & Albert Museum, London. Experts believe it was made in Syria in the 14th Century but of course we know it was made by the fairies.

The Penrith corpse road

A corpse road suitable for the whole family to walk

THIS is a corpse road that is not too long, family-friendly and comes with the added advantage of being close to the Rheged Discovery Centre. This visitor attraction has cafes, shops, galleries, a huge cinema and plenty of activities for children. You'll find it just off the A66 near J40 of the M6 at Penrith. You can also park on Redhills Lane beside Greggs and Burger King closer to the M6 roundabout. As with so many corpse roads, we know about this one because of a legal dispute. In 1945 the path was being fought over and its status as a corpse road was used to fight its corner. It began at the village of Sockbridge and led to St Andrew's Church in the centre of Penrith. There was also mention of this corpse road going to and being used by the Lowther family on their nearby estate. It's more practical to do this corpse road in reverse but the M6 roundabout means the path now stops at Skirsgill. You'll also find near here a large ancient standing stone unceremoniously tucked away on the industrial estate. Also nearby but on private land is a holy well.

THE WALK: To start this walk properly it's worth doubling back to Skirsgill. You may even wish to call and see the ancient Standing Stone. Follow the path through the gate and along a wooded lane to the railway tunnels. The path then drops gradually down towards the River Eamont. Cross the bridge and cut up through the field to Sockbridge. This

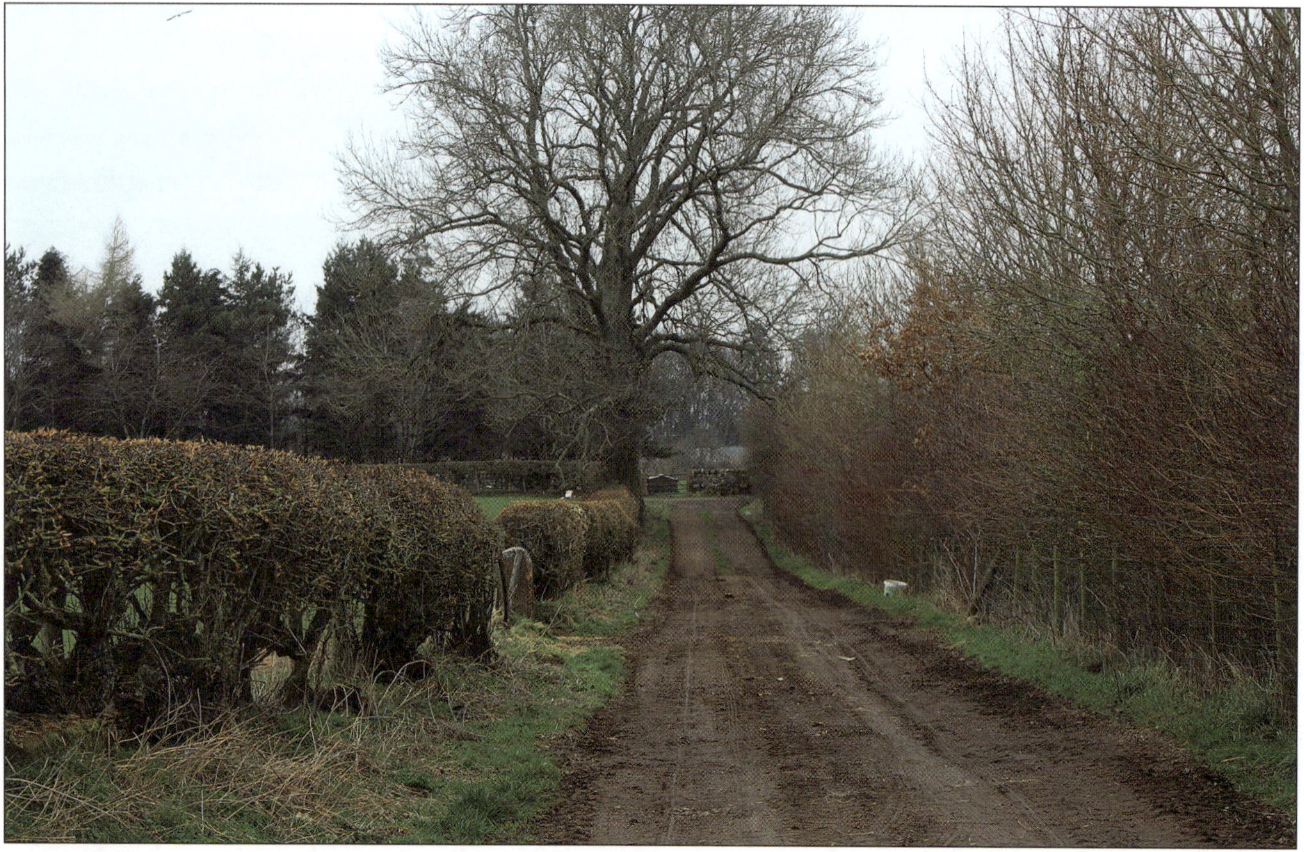

is a residential village but you may wish to stay and enjoy a lunch at the Queen's Head Inn before making your return.

NEARBY: Visit Rheged Discovery Centre. You are also close to Penrith which has plenty of shops including independent bookshops.

The corpse road as it enters the village of Sockbridge

Previous page: The Sockbridge to Penrith corpse road

> THERE is a note in the *Penrith Observer* of 6th February 1894: "Only once do I remember a funeral procession to have gone up Fell Lane, on its way to the Penrith Cemetery, and on that occasion some of the old folks in the town said it was curious that 'the proper corpse road' up Wordsworth Street was not taken." The mention of Wordsworth Street is interesting as it is known that victims of the plague of 1597 were buried on land known as Plague Lonning (or perhaps the lonning led to it) between Wordsworth Street and Graham Street. There was a local saying that this was a spot 'where the birds never sing'. The land has since been built on for housing.

214 : PENRITH   THE CORPSE ROADS OF CUMBRIA

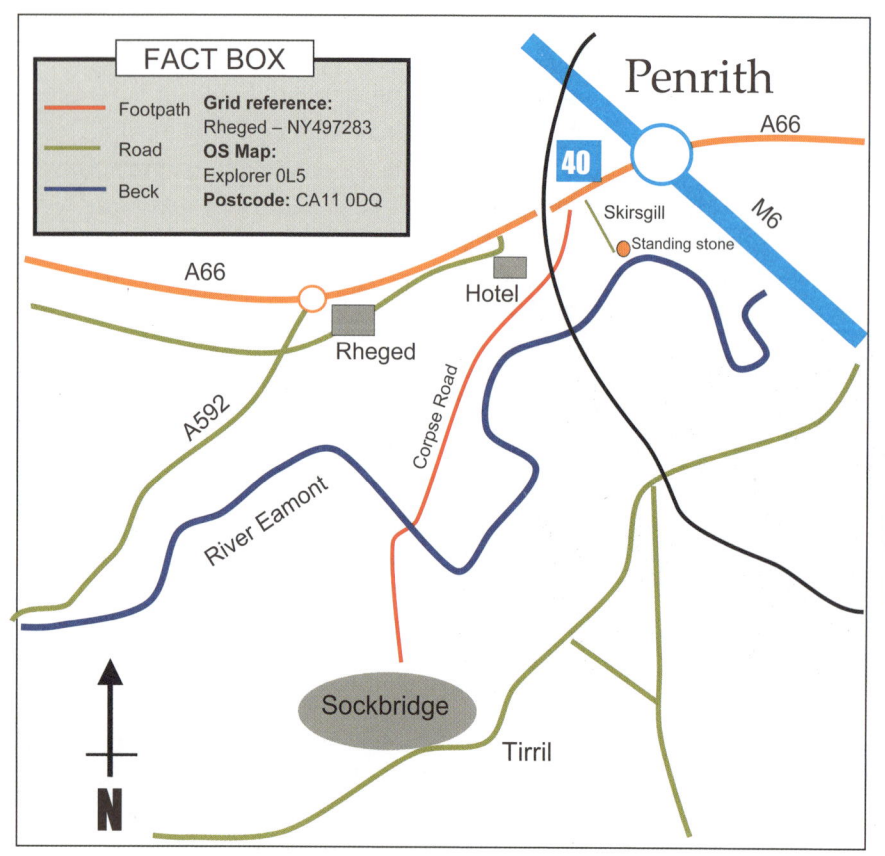

FACT BOX

- Footpath
- Road
- Beck

Grid reference: Rheged – NY497283
OS Map: Explorer OL5
Postcode: CA11 0DQ

Rather suggestive is this standing stone which lies just off the corpse road. Was it once a marker for the road? It's now tucked away rather unceremoniously on the Skirsgill industrial estate. Grid ref: NY509287

Last Writes

And now it's over to you...

"History, a distillation of rumour"

– **Thomas Carlyle**

WE hope you have enjoyed this look at the corpse roads of Cumbria and have had the opportunity to walk at least a couple of the paths mentioned.

These corpse roads are fortunately still public footpaths and make an enjoyable day out. We felt it important to record them before they were lost to history but we have also become convinced that there's another purpose to them: they are a potential economic boost for some of the less-visited parts of the county. The Lake District National Park has, of course, no difficulty in attracting tourists but those parts of the county outside the Park can struggle to woo holidaymakers away from honey-pots such as Keswick, Windermere or Coniston. That's a pity because these more rural parts of the county have a beauty of their own: the coastal paths in West Cumbria, the views over Morecambe Bay in the south or the stunning scenery around the Solway estuary are all worth venturing out to see. Corpse roads, and other historic paths, offer a 'carrot' to dangle in front of tourists to encourage them to go that extra mile. We have organised a few guided walks along the Irton corpse road, near Gosforth. This is a part of the county which tourists normally only dash through in their car on the way to Wasdale or Eskdale, but even on a wet or windy Monday morning we have seen 20 or 30 people turn up at Irton to find out more about the corpse roads there. They have visited the lovely St Paul's Church and put money into the donation box, walked the corpse road then had coffee or lunch at Irton Hall; it's a much-welcome economic boost to the area but has been achieved with minimal cost on publicity, simply relying on people's natural curiosity. It would be easy and relatively cheap to organise similar events at the many corpse roads elsewhere in the county. And

Tourists taking part in the Irton corpse road walks   *Picture: Angela Kirby*

given the millions invested in promoting the Lake District National Park, it would require only a small percentage of those funds switching to other parts of Cumbria to achieve the goal of giving the rest of the county an economic boost. It doesn't seem too much to ask.

THE CORPSE ROADS OF CUMBRIA

There is still much work to be done in cataloguing the corpse roads and the history behind them. We keep a note of any additional information that comes our way on a Google map (visit https://tinyurl.com/ybo9fojr) and are grateful to all those who contact us with corrections or details of other corpse roads (you can email us on alanjcleaver@gmail.com). It is our hope that local history societies will pick up the baton in many instances and investigate further but there's nothing to stop individuals lending a hand too.

Here are some suggestions as to how you can join in the exploration even if you have no previous experience of carrying out historical research. Simply speaking to villagers is a good place to start. Oral tradition has (as in the case of Bassenthwaite's corpse road) often provided a vital clue but it is good to also have any written evidence. The local archive office is the repository for historical documents but don't expect the archivist to just tap 'corpse road' into a computer and give you all the answers within a couple of minutes. There are hours of hard (but enjoyable) work ahead poring over historical records. The often self-published booklets on a village's history are a good place to start.

Team up with your local history society; they may have already researched the area's ancient paths including suggestions of corpse roads.

Once you have found a potential corpse road, it's time to put your boots on and start walking it. Watch out for any clues en route such as possible coffin rests or suggestive place names. Talk to farmers or those you meet on the path and ask them if they have heard of any history or

Our Google map of corpse roads

legends about the path being used in the past as a corpse road. Appealing on social media or through the local press can also prove fruitful.

Finally, do let us know your results and perhaps also send a letter to your local history society and archive office so they have a permanent record of your results. And do not feel left out if you live outside Cumbria. Corpse roads certainly existed elsewhere in Britain and they are waiting to be discovered.

To get you started here are some references we have hinting at corpse roads yet to be rediscovered. We have a couple of notes about corpse roads leading to Dalton or Ulverston in the south of the county. The first is from *Cumbrian Miscellany* published by Barrow Civic and Local History Society (no date but probably 1989) and written by Dennis Laird. It is also a widely-held oral tradition:

"As Walney was a 'chapel of ease' under the parish of Dalton, most burials took place at Dalton itself. There was a road used as a corpse road from North Scale township, which ran from the north of the settlement over Walney channel to the mainland near the settlement of Cocken."

The corpse road survives as a public footpath and goes through a railway tunnel, then past Ormsgill Farm. The current owners of the farm – Geoff and Anita Sharpe – have given us some valuable help in pursuing this further. They have also done much good work on protecting this and other public footpaths in the area from closure.

Not far from Dalton is the town of Ulverston and this too appears to have been a mother church at one time to rural parishes. There is mention in *From Track to Bypass* by Wilkinson of a corpse road leading from Coniston to Ulverston:

"Ulverston extended as far as Little Langdales and before Torver Chapel was erected all inhabitants of the district west of Coniston Lake had to carry the dead to Ulverston. The route generally followed was Coniston to Torver, past Stable Harvey and down the Crake Valley to Penny Bridge and so to Ulverston (there was a resting place at Jenkin Sike)."

His mention of Jenkin Sike (or syke) is interesting because of the anecdote (see page 138) that survives of a corpse being lost at this location. While the precise route is not specified, there is a footpath running through these locations which today is branded as part of the Cumbria Way. It could prove worthwhile for the people of Coniston and Ulverston to research this further and promote it as a corpse road. It is also worth mentioning that there are references to the people of Hawkshead taking their dead to Dalton for burial (see *The Book of Coniston* by WG Collingwood).

We also have a note from the *Manchester Times* of November 16th 1889 which is worth mentioning in respect of corpse roads in this south-western part of the county:

"A curious funeral incident is recorded by 'Wonderful' Walker who ministered so long at Seathwaite last century. 'The inhabitants' he says, 'were conveying a body from Seathwaite to Kirkby for interment, in the depth of winter, when the snow began to fall; by the time they had reached the hill above Newfield they could go no further with the body, and it was left on the common for a few days.' After this they sent a petition to Lord Derby, the lord of the manor, praying he would erect them a place of worship, and there are writings showing that the Earl built a chapel."

The authors Lesley Park and Alan Cleaver take a rest!

In 1957 the Women's Institutes in Cumbria joined together to produce a history of their villages. The results were published in a book, *From Some Westmorland Villages*, which is rich in local tales. Included is mention of a corpse road at Crosby Ravensworth which demands further investigation:

"Not so attractively named as some roads, but interesting in its implications, is Corpse Road, a track almost lost sight of now, but evidently at one time it led from Brackenslack by fields to Meaburn and then to Crosby church. It was the custom for a funeral coming this way to stop in Meaburn by the cross there, whilst the mourners, with heads uncovered, sang a hymn before finishing the journey to the church and cemetery."

Of particular interest is the mention of a cross at Meaburn (is it still there?) and the use of this spot to 'rest' and sing a hymn which echoes our suggestion of the real purpose of coffin rests.

Maulds Meaburn: On the route of the Crosby Ravensworth corpse road

It is both surprising and exciting how many new references to corpse roads in the county we still come across after almost three years of research. Some are vague, some are little more than a strongly-held personal belief but others hint at stronger roots and are worthy of further investigation. We make a note of most on our Google map in the hopes that others may come across corroborative evidence.

In addition to our research of corpse roads, we are investigating many of the county's other ancient tracks: the trods, lonnings, occupation roads and meanderings that criss-cross this beautiful part of the world. We will be publishing some of them shortly in a new book, *Get Lost*. Keep an eye out for it and join us as we continue to explore Cumbria's rich tapestry of footpaths.

You can follow Alan Cleaver on @thelonningsguy on Twitter for more corpse road updates.

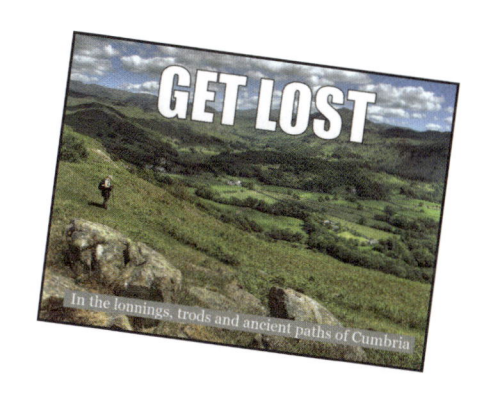

Watch out for our next book: *Get Lost - in the ancient trackways of the Lake District and Cumbria.*

Index

A
Aberdeen Evening Express 65
Alexander, William 175
Alston Moor 155, 164
Ambleside 22, 25, 29, 32, 33
Annales Caermoelenses, Or Annals of Cartmel 20, 136, 137
Appleby 12
Arlecdon 183
Armitt, Mary 25, 29, 31, 186
Arnside 206
Arval bread 189
Asquith, Roger Dr 50
Atkinson, Rev J C 34

B
Baddeley, MJB 20
Baines, Noel 9
Baingrigg 34
Ballad of Blind Charlie 100
Bampton 123
Barkbeth Farm 144, 146, 147
Barton 119
Bassenthwaite 144
Bassett, Elizabeth 204
Battle of the Way 116
Bees, Telling the 150
Beetham 204
Beetham Repository 206
Bell, Spencer 115
Bellman, The 162
Benson 34
Best, George 142
Bewcastle 200
Bidding 160
Bier 41, 138
Bigrigg 184
Binsey Link 175
Binsey Mission Community 175
Bishop of Carlisle 19
Bishop of Durham 156
Bogg, Edmund 98
Boggles 91, 120, 133
Boot Mill 8, 22
Bootle Parish Council 60, 61
Borrowdale 18, 115, 118
Bowthorn 184
Brackenhowe 124
Brackenslack 220
Brampton 87, 198
Brampton Old Church 198
Bridal paths 70
Bridle paths 70
Britain's Favourite View 22
British Newspaper Archive 56
Brocklebank, Thomas 58, 61, 77
Brownie 206
Brownrigg Farm 145
Burgess, Neil 183
Burne-Jones 68, 77
Burnmoor Tarn 8, 9
Burrough, Joseph 58, 61
Buttermere 174
Byers, Richard 90

C
Caine, Caesar 153, 156, 187
Caine, Hall 12, 13
Caldbeck 145

Calder Abbey 10, 183
Camerton 88
Camerton Ha' Boggle 91
Candlesnuff fungus 134
Cark 136
Carlisle Diocesan Conference 108, 142
Carruthers, Frank 53
Cartgate 6
Cartmel 137
Cartmel Church 137
Cartmel Commons' Enclosure
    Commissioners 138
Castle Sowerby 185
Castlerigg stone circle 104
Cat Bells, 113
Chambers, Therese 106, 107
Chapel Stile 29, 40, 43
Chapel Well 203
Chinese lanterns 142, 143
Christmas Day 71
Christmas Readings 41, 48
Church Lonning 9
Church of Grasmere, 31
Clare, John 200
Clarke, Sir Edward 62
Clarke's Survey of the Lakes 164
Cleator 154,185

Cleator Moor 107, 192
Clocks 108, 109
Coffin rests 178
    Crosslacon 182, 183, 184
    Egremont 187
    Fallen Cross 184
    Fawn Cross 185
    Grasmere 178, 180
    Lamplugh 181, 182
    St Bees 180
    Weeping Cross 186
Coin tree 39
Coltmoor Cross 188
Coniston 138
Corpse candles 67, 132
Corpse Cross 182, 185
Corpse drop 170, 171
Corpse stone 174, 179
Cow Lonning 181
Cowper HS 170
Crake Valley 218
Creep-i-th'-call Bridge 210
Crosby Ravensworth 220
Cross Fell 153
Cross Hill 88
Crosshill House 170
Crosthwaite 18, 98, 115

Crowe, Shelley 112
Cumberland and Westmorland
    Antiquarian and Archaeological
    Society 91, 109, 133
Cumberland Assizes 61
Cumberland Pacquet 56
Cumbria magazine 172, 204
Cumbria Way 116, 145
Cumbrian Miscellany 218
Cumrew 119
Curtains 111
Customs at death 110, 141, 142, 143,
    150, 157, 165, 190

D

Dalton 191, 218
Day, Justice 61
Death chair 87
Death Knell 107
Death knocks 119
Death lights 132
Death's door 163
Denham Tracts 152
Denman, Derek 51
Derwentwater 115
Devereux, Paul 204, 207
Devil's Bridge 184

Devil's door 71
Devon and Cornwall Notes
    and Queries 179
Diana, Princess of Wales 141
Dickens, Charles 189
Dickie Lonning 145, 148
Dickinson, William 152, 161
Dixies 207
Dixon, Thomas 184
Dobbie Bank 133
Dobbie Lane 133, 136
Double-backed bridge 8
Dove Cottage 24, 27
Down't Lonnin 48
Dugdale, Graham 204

E

Eden Hall 210
Egremont 180
Ellerclose 62, 63
Ellis, David Canon 163
Ellwood, Thomas 10
Embleton 175
Ennerdale Hotel 185, 187
Eskdale 7
Eskin Farm 174
Eslick, Barbara 111

Esmeralda 99
Ewart, Malcom 144
Eye-keld well 168

F

Faery tearoom 46
Fairer, Dr William 112
Fairies 210
Fairy steps 204, 205
Fallen Cross 184
Fangs Brow 52
Fawe Park 114, 116
Fell, John 191
Fell Lane 213
Fenton 196
Fiends Fell 153
Firbank 3
Flatt Lonning 145
Flookburgh 137, 138
Forty Years in a Moorland Parish 34
Foulshaw 207
Fox sisters 120
From Some Westmorland Villages 220
From Track to Bypass 218
Friars' Well 94
Frizington 182, 183
Funeral biscuits 190, 191

G

Gaitskill, Wm 63
Gallows Hill 85
Garner, Jas P 172
Garrigill 153
Gattenby, Kelly-ann 111
George, Ron 174
Get Lost 221
Ghosts
    Caldbeck white lady 145
    Camerton 91
    Corby 91
    Irton 64
    Loweswater 53
    Park End Road 91
    Wasdale 12
    Workington Hall 91
Gibson, Alexander Craig 138
Goggleby Stone 124, 128
Goodwin, Harry 36
Google corpse road map 217
Gosforth 192
Graham, Jeni 112
Graham Street 213
Grasmere Journals 185
Great Lonning 85
Green Lane 137, 138

Greenlands 72
Greystoke 163, 165
Guardian, The 142

H

Hadrian's Wall 203
Hallsenna 85
Harcourt, Dora 71, 108, 151, 161
Harrison family 32
Harrison, Richard 148
Haweswater reservoir 122
Hawkshead 33, 170, 219
Hawkshead Hill 171
Hayton 195
Hazelslack Tower 209
Headless Cross 139, 140
Helena Thompson Museum 94
Helm Wind 153, 155
Hesket 108
Hexham, Battle of 64
High Court 68
High Nook Farm 50
High Rigg 99
Hills WH 34
Hob-thross 206
Hodgson, Levi 34
Hodgson, 'Putty Joe' 12
Hogarth Mission 120

Holme Wood 50, 51
Holme, John 124
Holmrook Hall 62, 77
Holy well, Grasmere 32, 35, 186
How Stone 34, 186
How, The 196
How Top 29, 34
Huddleston, Squire 169
Hughes, Pauline 111
Huntingstile 29, 41, 47
Huntsman Inn 10
Hurtleton 201, 202
Hutton John 169
Hutton, Rev William 206

I

Irthington 201, 202
Irton Hall 58, 61
Irton Oak 64, 66
Irton, John 64
Isle of Man 13
Ivison HC 53

J

Jackson, Herbert and Mary 120
Jackson, W 91
Jenkin Syke 138, 219
Johnby 163

Jones, John Paul 20
Jopson 138
Jordan's Cross 188
Justice Joyce 68

K

Keld 109, 124
Kelsick 172, 175
Kelsick Farm 174
Kemble, Rev Mr 108, 148, 150, 162
Kennedy, Rosina 107
Keswick, 114
Keswick Footpath Preservation
    Society 116
Killington 3
Kinder Scout 114
King Henry VI 64
King Richard I 88
King Richard II 90
Kirk Trods 196
Kirkby 218
Kirkby Lonsdale 3, 184 193
Kirkby Stephen 87
Kirkland 153
Kirkstile Inn 55

L

La'al Ratty 22

Laird, Dennis 218
Lamplugh, Lady Ann 64
Lancashire Evening Post 67, 133
Langdale 31
Langdale Gate 32
Latrigg 114
Laversdale 201
Laying out 109
Leper's Door 43
Lifting the corpse 107, 161, 162, 190
Liggin Kessin 159
Ling Fell 172
Little Langdale 32
Little Lonning 85
Liverpool Daily Post 185
Longrigg 199
Lore of the Land 135
Lorton & Derwent Fells Local History Society 57
Lorton Church 172
Loughrigg 32
Loughrigg and Beneath-Moss 31
Loughrigg Cross 188
Lovers Lonning 181
Loweswater 50, 182
Lowther Castle (Whitehaven) 6
Luck of Eden Hall 210
Lutwidge 77
Lutwidge Arms 81

M

Maggie's Lonning 52, 56
Manchester Guardian 114
Manchester Times 219
Mardale 122, 124, 131
Marshall, Betty 181, 193
Matterdale 167
Maulds Meaburn 220
Mean, Angela Parker 111
Mickle Langdale 32
Middleton, George 35
Mill Fields 90, 95
Millican, Thomas 156
Millom 206
Mirehouse family 57
Mirrors 108, 110
Morecambe Bay 206
Morris, William 77
Myerside 138
Mysterious Britain 7

N

Nab Oak 36
Nab Scar 28
Nab Well, 28, 35, 36

Naddle, The 100
Neasham, George 160, 168
Nether Wasdale 17, 19, 20
Newcastle Chronicle 180
Newfield 218
Nichols 32

O

Old Coach Road, 167
Old Hell Way 209
Old Wall 202
Ormsgill Farm 218
Orton 112, 135
Overthwaite 206

P

Packhorse Ways 62
Pae, Josephine 110
Page, Jim Taylor 124, 163
Pallaflat 188
Palmer, William T 152, 180, 185, 193
Parker CA, Dr 64, 187, 188
Path problems 69
Pembrokeshire 171
Penfold, Henry 109, 119, 133, 181, 195, 199, 202
Pennine Way 159

Penrith 211
Penrith Cemetery 213
Penrith Observer 213
Petition 3
Pikeside 5
Plague Lonning 213
Portinscale 118
Powley, Mary 155
Puckle, Bertram 190
Punch magazine 116

Q
Queen's Guide to the Sands 207
Queen's Head, Sockbridge 213

R
Ramblers 69, 116, 145
Rawnsley, Rev Hardwicke 116
Redgill 112
Rheda 184
Rheged 211
Richardson, John 107, 162
Ritson, Old Will 10
River Bela 207
River Eamont 211
River Irt 80
River Kent 206

Robinson, Cedric 207
Robinson, Charles 100
Rollinson, William 189
Roman Walk 202
Rosthwaite 115
Rottington 187
Row Bridge 22
Rowan 12
Rowland, J 51
Rum butter 191
Rushbearing 33
Rycroft, Stephen 98
Rydal-and-Loughrigg 31
Rydal Hall 24
Rydal Mount 24, 26, 35

S
Salt 109, 111
Sanctuary Stone 169
Sandside 206, 207
Scroggs 202
Seacross Lonning 177
Seathwaite 219
Seaton Mill 96
Sebergham, 162
Shadow of a Crime 13
Shap 122
Shap Heritage Centre 127

Shap Local History Society 123
Sharpe, Geoff and Anita 218
Shee, QC 61
Shy signpost 52
Simpson, Jacqueline 135
Simpson, Revd Canon James 87
Skelly, John 110, 192
Skelwith Bridge 33
Skirsgill 211
Smith, Joe 111
Smith, Susan 63
Sod of earth 109
Sorrowstones 187
Spiller's Stone 165
Spiritualism 120
Spitting Stone 148
Splitfoot, Mr 120
Squeezed Gut Lonning 85
St Andrew's, Greystoke 163
St Andrew's, Penrith 211
St Andrew's, Rosthwaite 115
St Batholomew, Loweswater 52, 55
St Bees 10, 170,186
St Bega's holy well, 186
St Catherine's, Eskdale 21
St Catherine's well 9, 10, 22
St Cuthbert's, Lorton 173
St Cuthbert's Well, 210

St John holy well 99
St John's Cross 206, 207
St John's in the Vale, 98 101
St John's, Garrigill 157
St Kentigern, Caldbeck 145
St Kentigern, Irthington 203
St Lawrence the Martyr, Kirkland 159
St Martin's, Brampton 198
St Mary's Hayton, 196
St Mary's, Stapleton 199
St Michael's, Beetham 207
St Michael's Chapel, St Bees, 186
St Michael's, Nether Wasdale, 19
St Michael's, Shap 123
St Olaf's, Wasdale 18, 22
St Oswald's, Grasmere 25
St Paul's, Irton 60, 75
St Peter's, Camerton 97
Stable Harvey 218
Sockbridge 211
Stadle Dykes 145
Stained glass 77
Standing Stone, Skirsgill 211
Stapleton 199
Stock Bridge 82, 84, 86
Stockdale, James 136, 137, 138
Storth 206
Sty Head Pass 15

Sunderland Daily Echo 41
Swindale Head 121, 122, 128, 129
Syke 138

T
Tailbert 124
Tardis coffin 142
Tawney Boy 206
The Book of Coniston 219
Thirlmere 99
Thomas, Taffy 48
Thompson, Lesley 112
Thorne, Nick 138
Torver 138, 218
Town End 34
Tripadvisor 194
Troutbeck 162
Tumban, Wm 63

U
Ulpha 5
Ulverston 33, 138, 218

V
Vaux, Tony 145
Victoria and Albert Museum 210
Victoria History of Cumberland 155

Vineyard 62

W
Wainwright, Alfred 50
Walker, Richard 63
Wallace, Doreen 133
Wallace, William 153, 155, 164
Walney 218
Wasdale 7, 18
Wasdale Head Inn 8, 10
Waverley Hotel, 194
Weeping Cross 186
Westwood, Jennifer 135
Whellan, William 88, 184
Whinfield, Myles and Tamar 5
White Moss 29
Whitehaven 6, 20, 71, 108, 120, 161, 194
Whitehaven Herald 5, 6
Whitehaven News 132
Widecombe-in-the-Moor 179
Will o the Wisp 135, 136
Wilson Planting 174
Wishing Gate Road 34
Witherslack 206, 207
Withnail and I, 127
Wonderful Walker 219

Woodall, Pamela 111
Woodruff, Derek 90
Wordsworth, Dorothy 26, 185
Wordsworths 24, 25, 35
Wordsworth Street, Penrith 213
Workington 88
Workington Hall 90
Wreay Cottage 46
Wren, Keith 99
Wrigley, George Rev'd 41
Wythburn Church 99
Wythop 174

XYZ
Xylaria hypoxylon 134

PRINTED IN CUMBRIA

Printed by H&H Reeds of Penrith